WISDOM

FROM

OTHERS

Life Lessons from Loss

Donita M. Brown

& Others

DARR, LLC

SPRINGFIELD, TN

DARR

Springfield, TN 37172

www.donitabrown.com

Library of Congress Cataloging-in-Publication Data

Brown, Donita M.

ISBN 978-1-7340261-0-8

Printed in the United States of America

1 2 3 4 5 6 7 8 9 10

Contents

Preface

Thank you for picking up this book. Whether this book was suggested to you by a friend, given to you after you suffered a loss, or you found it and bought it because of the title, I'm glad you are here.

This book is a compilation of stories told by twelve different authors about a loss they endured. Some of the losses are tragic, some were life-changing, one was funny, but all will touch your heart. Each of these lessons from with a bit of wisdom from the loss.

The Introduction, written by a friend of mine, David Archer. David had the original idea for this book. After my first book came out, Wisdom From Others: 9 Life Lessons From My Dad, David approached me about writing a book on loss. On David's 50th birthday, he lost his son to cancer.

The idea of writing a book on loss was not an idea that I initially wanted to pursue. Writing about loss book seemed too hard to write, too emotional, too raw. For a few months after that discussion, the idea of writing the book kept coming back to me. I met people who had faced a significant loss, and through that loss, had the wisdom to share. Finally, I decided to write the book when a friend of mine lost her mom unexpectedly. However, when writing about loss, there is a healing that occurs for the writer. In sharing the story of the loss may provide hope and solace for those who are experiencing a similar loss.

We all have faced loss, but through that loss, something else is gained. One of the best parts about writing my first book was to have someone tell me that they remember a piece of advice they remembered from their Dad. Then writing a book with my sister was so much more vibrant because there's strength in forming bonds with others.

Introduction

Jason had just turned eighteen years old. He was enjoying life as a senior in high school. Then he received the most challenging news that most of us could receive: he was diagnosed with terminal cancer. Mere months later, the disease would take his body, but it never took his spirit.

Humans have an incredible capacity to experience love, as well as loss, very profoundly. All of us, at different times in our lives, must face the pain of loss. That loss can come in many various forms. Loss is never easy to withstand, but how we deal with the pain of loss helps to define our character.

Loss is a crucible in which our faith and our joy are tested. Sometimes the testing seems to be more than we can handle, and we may need to depend on the support of others to help us cope.

This book is a collection of stories from many individuals that have faced different types of loss. Each author tells their story how they dealt with loss and how it helped shape their character.

Every day we wish we had one more day with Jason, even one more hour. But we know that we will see him again. We believe our experience of loss, while the most painful experience of our lives, has continued to build in us a higher capacity to demonstrate compassion for those around us who are also experiencing loss in their lives.

We sincerely hope this book touches yours.

David and Pam Archer

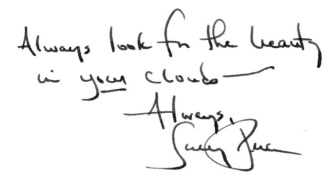

Always look for the beauty in your clouds —
Always,
Sarey Pue

The Addition of Clouds

Terry Price

I remember that evening in March 2016, looking out over our fields and knowing that the sunset would be special. So I grabbed my camera and wandered out among the curious horses and waited. I needed the time to myself. At that moment, I needed beauty.

As a photographer, **I've learned over the years that it's actually not just the sun that makes a beautiful sunset, but the addition of clouds.** To really have the spectrum of colors and textures in the sky, the fading sunlight needs something to catch or diffuse the light. That night the clouds were gorgeous — just waiting to be the canvas on which this sunset would be painted.

I composed, metered, focused, breathed, and took a few shots. Then I put the camera down and just took it all in. It was one of the loveliest sunsets I had ever seen

— from rich, dark blues and purples to rose and yellow on swirling clouds.

But then, color gave way to darkness. My phone rang--it was my Dad's caregiver from his assisted living facility, telling me my father had just passed away.

In the end, it was his kidneys that failed and not the dementia that pulled him under. And while a small consolation, we were grateful that Dad still knew us at the end, grateful that he regained consciousness one last time and talked with us before entering hospice and palliative care.

We had spent Dad's last day at his facility; him sleeping easily, and the rest of us carrying on conversations.

We would get up occasionally to check on him while hospice tracked his vitals and updated us. He had not spent a night alone for many months as we took turns, but this night his caregiver offered to stay and sent the rest of us home about dinner time. I did not know it was his last day. Nor did I figure out until later that he was leaving our horizon at the time I was photographing what I now realize was *his* sunset.

Unless the context jogs my memory, I never think of him as my stepfather. He was just Dad. I never knew my birth father, whose relationship with my Mom was a marital *Dr. Jekyll and Mr. Hyde* -- when he was sober he was kind and funny and lovable, especially to Mom. But when he drank, he became physically and emotionally abusive to her, and I grew up with stories that she put up with it. Finally, she left him for good when she feared that, while drunk, he might injure my little brother or me. He died a few years later leaving me with only a black and white memory of him that I'm still not sure was real or from a photograph.

Mom then met the only Dad I've ever known. And while he was always kind and generous, we didn't really become close until after I married and moved from home. At that point, our stepfather-stepson relationship softened, and the "steps" were removed. He didn't give a lot of advice but was always there to help me keep things in perspective. I would complain about a car repair or needing an appliance replaced, and his response was always, "Just be glad you have the money to do it, son." And most of the time I didn't have the money, but I knew what he was saying, learned from it, and stopped complaining.

Right after Dad retired, Mom learned she had ovarian cancer. She initially beat it, but it would return, and circumstances were such that when she was hospitalized in early September of 1994, Dad moved in and stayed with her for the five months and six unsuccessful surgeries. She passed away there with Dad by her side. He had left a handful of times to go home and check on things but never spent a night away from the love of his life.

Sometime after her death, my wife and I joined in with Dad and built him a cabin out behind our house, and he lived there until the dementia required the care of an assisted living facility. He became "Pa" to our children and their children. At his funeral visitation, a friend expressed their sympathy and I told them that he loved everyone, was loved by everyone, and spent right up until the last two years of his life doing things he loved to do, including riding his tractors and taking care of his longhorn cattle, which were really his pets.

The loss of a parent is a watershed moment for most of us, even if unrecognized at the time of passing. I felt untethered as I had helped Dad take care of himself and his affairs for the twenty-some years since Mom's passing. My mother had had the reputation of taking care of everyone else, even Dad, and at her passing, that role seemed to fall to me and so taking care of Dad was as natural as breathing. Even so, I was still his child, and he was still my father.

After Dad's passing, we took care of all the arrangements, took care of his final bills and shared the things he had left behind, and began to move forward with our lives without this caring, gentleman.

But after all of the details had been handled, I began to suffer from anxiety, which was a new experience for me. I tried to be patient, realizing that we all had been stretched to the limits, physically, emotionally, and spiritually, during the last eighteen months of his life. But the anxiety would not leave.

Eventually, I made an appointment with my family physician, a trusted friend who is a throwback to the doctors I grew up with - someone who knows you, your family, and is generous with his time. He was also Dad's physician and my wife and I had brought Dad to see him countless times over the previous few years, and he was well aware of everything.

As we visited, his kind eyes and knowing nod comforted me as I shared. When I had finished with my symptoms and experiences, he took a deep breath and said I was both grieving and going through a crisis of control. And the moment he said it, I felt it was right.

> *"You've pretty much been able to take situations and handle them. You've made decisions, experienced the consequences, changed directions, but somehow most always, you've maintained control. With your Dad, you did everything you could. You consulted with doctors and hospitals, made treatment plans and carried them through, and yet he still passed away. There are some things that are beyond our control, and this was one of them. Part of you is grieving a loss, but another part is grieving that you failed him. But you didn't. There are always going to be things beyond our control, no matter how hard we try. That's just life."*

I took the wisdom in, but it's not a quick fix to learn and incorporate. As time passed I worked through my lessons.

Sometimes coming to grips with loss is a matter of coming to grips with our own fallibility. Sometimes coming to grips with the loss of a loved one is a matter of coming to grips with our own mortality and the sense that we've lost the love extended to us.

Mythologist and storyteller, Michael Meade, says that death is not the opposite of life but rather the opposite of birth. *Birth and death are both aspects of life.* There is life long before our first cry and after our last breath. Life always *is.* Birth and death are just the bookends to this physical body we borrow for a bit. I have learned that it is the same with love.

Life can be like the sun in that a sunrise begins when we first see the glow over the horizon, the birth of a new day. Sunset is when it leaves us again, and the stars fill the sky. Between the sunset and the sunrise, the sun is always there, even when we cannot see it.

After Mom passed away, Dad grieved and asked me why it hurt so much. I told him that I believe that the amount of pain experienced is equal to the amount of love shared. I asked if he would have loved less if he could hurt less now? "No," he firmly answered. Then we must learn to remember the depth of the love and how it will always last, even when we cannot see the object of our love, long after the pain lessens.

DONITA M. BROWN & OTHERS

There shall always be the sun. That's just a part of the big, beautiful sky under which we live and love. But there are things we can't control any more than we can control the sun. Sometimes magic in life comes from just letting go and finding the rhythm in our breath and our life. Sometimes magic in life is found in the clouds.

We are made to love and to be loved with all the highs and inherent complications and losses we cannot control. Sometimes the best we can do is to live and immerse ourselves in the awe of it all, with gratitude, and find that the essence of both love and life always has been and always shall be.

TERRY PRICE

Terry Price, is a Tennessee based writer, creative coach, Certified Veriditas trained labyrinth facilitator, and photographer, with an MFA in writing from Spalding University in Louisville. He is a former Program Director and current mentor in MTSU Write (formerly The Writer's Loft) creative writing program at Middle Tennessee State University. (www.mtsu.edu/write). He works with creatives one-on-one and leads workshops and retreats including retreats on an introduction to and using the labyrinth as both a spiritual and creative tool.

A self-described lifestyle photographer, his portfolio includes street, landscape, and travel photography and his current traveling exhibit features work from Italy in an ekphrastic collaboration with twenty of Tennessee's best poets. He is currently shooting travel photos for a major ekphrastic exhibit and book of photos and poetry. His photos have accompanied pieces in various journals, newspapers, and magazines and sold to individuals.

You can learn more about Terry through his website www.terryprice.net

I Am Not Perfect, But I Am Good Enough

Frannie Bryson

Through the heart-wrenching experience of losing my good friend and gaining a son, I have learned that you don't have to always be perfect or have all the answers. You must simply be willing to put in the effort and love wholeheartedly. **I am not perfect, but I am good enough.**

On June 3, 2017, at 9:40 am John Robert Sanders, known by most as JR, lost his temper while commuting to work. He was on his motorcycle on Briley Parkway in Nashville, Tennessee. His commute ended as he died in a horrific collision with an 18-wheeler.

JR was 20 years old and just a few months away from marrying the love of his life and the mother of his 9-month-old son, John Robert, Junior. He was the person who exuded energy and always looked for a good laugh. He was the life of the party and the sort of individual that made everyone feel special even if they'd only spoken once.

JR was only about 5'5" and weighed about 120 lbs, but because of his high energy and a larger-than-life personality, people often overlooked his small stature. He was a mechanic by trade, fearless and especially adventurous on anything with wheels. I had witnessed him do countless dangerous things in a vehicle, and while he always pulled them off without a hitch, his luck would eventually run out.

JR's young son, JJ, was only 5 months old when JR decided to purchase a motorcycle. He and his fiancée Zoiey would often ride together, but they knew the gravity of these rides. They appointed Godparents for JJ on the slim chance that something were to happen to them. This is where I come in. I am Frannie DiGiovanni, and my Fiance Ben and I are JJ's Godparents. Zoiey and JR were our best friends, and because neither of them had close relationships with their families, they asked that we take sole custody of JJ if ever anything happened to them. Now when I say "best friends" I don't mean the casual kind of friendship where you only spend time together at special functions or catch up occasionally on the weekend. The four of us spent at least 3 nights a week and every weekend together just living life and planning out our futures. The boys were often dreaming of new trucks, motorcycles, and boats while Zoiey and I combed Pinterest for wedding ideas and DIY home decor projects. At the time, none of us had our own homes, and we weren't even close to being financially stable enough to buy new trucks, but when you are young, you can always dream.

Losing JR was a heartache like no other and the way he passed just exacerbated the hurt even further. During the first few months after he died, I kept busy by supporting Zoiey and taking over almost all parental responsibilities because she was simply too lost in sorrow to try to care for her 9-month-old baby. I can still remember feeling stricken and overwhelmed as I stood next to Zoiey and JR's family in the funeral reception line.

Zoiey was not comfortable around JR's family, and most of the visitors were people who had known JR before he'd started his life with Zoiey, so she knew very few of them. They would all say how sorry they were and how they were praying for her and try to hug her. The never-ending line of mourners drained Zoiey, quiet and shy as she was. It was at that moment that I first had the thought of "How will I ever be good enough?" Standing next to my friend's casket as the sea of strangers rushed forward to bombard us with sympathy, I felt as if I could never support Zoiey the way she needed or be a good enough Godmother for JJ. In hindsight, I realize that during that first moment of self-doubt, when I felt fragile and completely without ability was when God began doing His best work in me. Sometimes power can only be made perfect in our weakness. Not strength! **I am not perfect, but I am good enough.**

Had I not been so emotionally drained and sad, I would have not been looking for anything good.

I have learned in life that your family is not just the people you were born to but those that love you unconditionally.

Although I didn't give birth to JJ, I had loved him since before he was born and for me, he will always be my baby. This isn't a feeling that came from losing JR but because JR and Zoiey were my dear friends for many years and we always supported each other like family. I was still very involved with my Godson so later in the summer when JJ's 1st birthday arrived. I had the party perfectly planned and a whole slew of fun decorations at the ready. I knew this party wouldn't take the pain and discomfort of JR's passing away, but I felt that JJ should not miss out on anything he would have had with JR and so party we did. The initial shock of JR's passing had mostly worn off, and people had tried to make awkward encounters with Zoiey or I better with humor. There were lots of comments like "Wow Frannie you're such a good Dad" or "You and Zoiey take such great care of JJ, y'all almost seem like a lesbian couple." While they shared all these comments with good intentions, they only added to my feeling of inadequacy. I was doing all I could to make sure JJ's life stayed as normal and healthy as possible while encouraging Zoiey and trying to keep my own spirits up. No matter what I did, I would never be good enough and I was always failing in some area. During JJ's party, we had food, cake, and opened gifts. While opening gifts, I held JJ and Zoiey unwrapped the presents and showed each to the small crowd of family and friends. Again I felt as though I could never be good enough. Sitting in front of a large room full of people trying to fill the void left by the devastating loss of JR.

I am not perfect, but I am good enough.

No matter how much I loved and cared for JJ, I would never be JR. While this made me feel inadequate, I learned that I need not be the same parent as him to be doing a good job of loving and providing for JJ. Just because I don't know precisely how to handle every situation or correctly navigate the struggles of life does not mean I am failing. **I am not perfect, but I am good enough**. Was I prepared to be a second mother to the most wonderful boy in the world? No. Am I qualified to help raise a tiny headstrong little boy into an adult? NO! But God would not have taken my friend from this earth and given me this burden to bear if I wasn't capable. I have had to learn, grow, and adapt during these last 2 years, and it has been complicated. These years have made me a better and more compassionate person. I have learned you don't have to be perfect, you must be willing to put in the effort life often demands and love wholeheartedly. If God calls you to it, he will grow you into who you need to be.

You do not have to be good at everything or have all the answers, but in your weakness, you can grow into a stronger, better, more capable person than you ever dreamed. God doesn't always call the qualified, he often qualifies the called.

JR lived life to the fullest and loved every experience and was a person without reserve. He always believed in himself, and while he was not gifted with all the necessary skills for success through hard work and an open heart, JR accomplished a significant amount in just 20 years of life. While I know that I am not nearly as fearless as he was, I am good at things he was not and can use my talents to help take care of my friend and Godson. I am not perfect, but I am good enough.

The feeling of inadequacy has always been a personal struggle of mine. After losing my friend, I could learn from these feelings. Looking back, I realize that if I had focused too heavily on being perfect during my childhood, I would have never become the person I am today. When I was 7 years old, my younger sister began to learn the fiddle, and I started playing the guitar. While I was doing well, my sister was more naturally gifted than I so she excelled much faster than I did. I had to put in twice as much effort, and often I still didn't sound as good as my sister. I was often bitter about this and began to develop the attitude of "I can't do it, so I just won't try."

My parents never accepted that excuse and despite my resistance made me keep playing guitar and broadening my musical horizons.

Fast forward to today, I am a full-time music instructor, and I teach guitar, fiddle, mandolin, ukulele, dobro, and bass. I also teach clogging lessons and coach a square dance team with my sister as my co-coach. These things were skills I once thought I was incapable of and not naturally gifted enough for. While a few years ago, I wasn't qualified to give lessons on any of them; through hard work, dedication, and an open heart, I became a very skilled musician and an even better teacher. I bring a unique perspective to learning a musical instrument, and I can help others who struggled like I once did because I can empathize with them in a way more naturally talented instructors cannot. If I had stayed stuck in the need to be *perfect* and quit playing music, I could not encourage others and inspire people the way I do today. **I am not perfect, but I am good enough.**

FRANNIE BRYSON

Frannie is a music teacher, traveler and lover of all things. She currently lives in Robertson County, TN, where she and her husband purchased their first home. When Frannie is not working, you can find her spending time with her family, scrapbooking, and playing music. She also LOVES to travel! She tries to explore a new destination every other month and in 2019 alone, she has visited 8 beautiful vacation spots. She believes that you will never wish for more money or junk when you are old, but rather will have wished for places to travel. Many people however mourn the dreams they didn't chase and the experiences they never had. Frannie tries to live every moment with intent and inspire others in the process.

Thanks for
your support!
Mark Cummings
aka Dad

I Thought It Would Last Forever

Mark Cummings

My cell phone buzzed in my pocket, and I listened to a voice mail. I had to sit down. It was as if someone had punched me in the gut. My friend Jackie asked if I was alright. "I'm okay." My wife and I were at a lovely wedding reception in 2017, socializing and eating snacks and having a good time. The happy couple was inviting everyone in for dinner, and this was not about me. I would deal with it later.

The message was from an old friend from my East High School days. "Mark, it's been torn down." A little piece of my soul died at that moment. The old house did not belong to me anymore, but it was **supposed to last forever – and I thought it would.** My parents had sold the Eastland house twenty years earlier, so the new owner could do whatever they pleased. I was supposed to strike it rich and buy it back and turn it into a museum, or remodel it and move back in, or turn it into a rental property. None of those things happened.

Why did I care anyway? Because it connected almost every memory of my childhood to that house. My brother and I would play a game in the yard we called "Mack and Joe." We were pretending to be other people, and we chose those names because they sounded tough. Our yard was a jungle for adventures.

Along with my sister, the three of us wrote our initials in the concrete when we got the new driveway. Dad saved up for years for that driveway project. He was so proud. We felt like we moved up three or four notches in the world because we had a concrete driveway. This was not just a house. It was my home.

Maybe David was mistaken, and it was another house in the neighborhood. After all, it was dark and perhaps he got it mixed up. It took forty-five minutes from the wedding reception, but I felt like I had to drive over late that night to see it with my own eyes. Jean, my wife, nodded off in the passenger seat. We drove down Eastland Avenue. When did these new stop signs go in?

"Jean, wake up. Look." A colossal machine was standing there in the dark, triumphant in its accomplishment, tearing down a perfectly good house order. I hated that machine and had to look away. Maybe a drive around the block would help, as I made a noise between hyperventilating and choking. Coming back around, it was still a pile of bricks and wood and huge stones from the foundation. The yard looked strangely small as if it were not big enough for the big old house that was a part of me.

The thing is, this house was not like any other house. It was built from materials from a mansion that had been torn down in downtown Nashville. The floor joists were closer together than other homes, just to make it stronger. Both my father and grandfather worked on building the house — **I thought it would last forever**.

When my parents were married in 1948, this was their home out in the country. If you were going east on Eastland, it was the last house on the left. Beyond that was farmland, all the way to the Cumberland River. So it really was out in the country. It's hard to imagine that today, with the hundreds of homes in that area.

This was the home where my parents brought home three children to raise. This was the home where I hid Oreos under my bed in a jar, so I could snack in the middle of the night. This was the home where I tried to build my own amplifier, and in the process burned up a microphone and almost electrocuted myself. This was the home with an upstairs apartment that provided a charming place for several small families to live over the years until three teenagers took it over.

Now the hardwood floors were gone. The double doors between the main hallway and the dining room were gone. All those glass doorknobs, the telephone shelf in the front hall, the handrail I would use to see how many stairs I could jump over, the closet upstairs I used as a clubhouse, all gone. Looking at the pile of rubble, I felt like I should get out of the car and salute.

Instead, I just said, "Well done, old friend. And goodbye."

Everyone and everything has a life cycle. An old mansion was torn down, which was home to other families before the materials were used for our house. Sixty-nine years later, our old house was torn down, and two brand new houses have been built in its place. They even removed that beautiful concrete driveway. Another casualty was the rock wall on the other side of the property. It was about two-and-a-half-feet high and was perfect for getting started on a bike that was too big for a boy, or for flying through the air on a sled.

This entire episode was painful for me; there is no denying that. The pain was real and went to my core. Being sentimental is a problem; I admit it. You would think it would generate a lot of pleasure, but it can be a windfall of misery.

Thousands of details about that house are etched into my memories, and so it lives on inside me. As I write these words for you to enjoy, I can close my eyes and walk across those hardwood floors, or look at our aluminum Christmas tree, or listen to the hum of the window fan upstairs during a sweltering summer night.

Two new families will be happy in their new homes and will have their own memories for years to come. **I thought our house would last forever**, and perhaps those new houses will never be torn down. I had to let it go.

Mark Cummings

Mark Cummings grew up in Nashville, Tennessee, in a home surrounded by love and support. His family was not dysfunctional, and he was never mistreated. This is significant because so many of his friends and extended family did not grow up this way. His childhood and adult life, while perhaps boring to some, provided Mark with the inspiration for his book published in 2018, "I Thought It Would Last Forever." In spite of his good fortune, Mark faced adversity at many points of his life, and the short story in this book illustrates one of those episodes. After working and retiring from a large telecommunications company, Mark continues to work as a telecom consultant. He has been married to his wife, Jean, for thirty-seven years, and they have two grown children and one granddaughter.

Same Company Forever

Donita M. Brown

Sitting in my office, the sound of silence deafened me that evening. The office was usually humming with the sound of a gigantic printer my team had renamed Clifford after the beloved Big Red Dog many of us grew up reading about or watching on TV, but I had to take a moment and turn away from my computer, and I turned off the printer. During the day our office was a flurry of activity. Never a dull moment in the large, oddly shaped, white building full of technology workers where we worked for a large health care company in Nashville, Tennessee.

The evenings were my favorite time in the office. During the day meetings often distracted me, but in the evenings I could concentrate and get what I thought was my "real work" completed. I spent a lot of my good working time in the office when everyone had gone home to their families. At this time in my life, I had not been blessed with children. My husband was often working a different shift than I was and we were the stereotypical workaholic couple with no kids. I knew there was more to life than working, but I just hadn't found it yet.

I loved to hear the hum of the printer, printing out sheets of paper. The rhythmic sound of page by page printing and the warmth of the sheets as they were spat out of the printer. Budgets and project plans and to-do lists were my favorite. Yet, there was something missing. I knew I was working for an extraordinary company, not just a great company, a truly remarkable one. But I felt a tug at my heart I couldn't explain. Shouldn't I work here forever? Wasn't that the plan? Success seemed to me to be to get a good job after college and work there until retirement. Wasn't that the plan I needed to follow?

Using an absurd amount of paper and printed reports, I would send daily reports highlighting budgets and errors and ways we could do things better. I could rattle off numbers for nearly anything budget-related like it was a second language and I was its professor. Often in the evenings, in the office's quiet, I would deliver these printed reports to the Directors who would report on the numbers later in the week. My gift to them was adorning these reports with hand-written sticky notes, hoping to give them some insight into their budget numbers.

I printed these reports at least once a week and sometimes more if we were in a difficult budget season or had important meetings coming up or if I just felt they needed it. It was an honor to put these reports in their office chairs. Often when I placed their statements in their chairs, I would linger in their offices, wondering what it was like to be in their position. At the time I was an analyst, just an ordinary number cruncher.

At this moment though, none of this mattered, my heart was aching, and I couldn't figure out why. I was turned away from my computer screen, catching my breath and trying to readjust my sails. I was looking at my whiteboard, something all IT professionals love to do.

Writing my to-do list, typically an easy task, became complex. I was overloaded and burdened. I could see my scales toppling over with each new task I needed to add.

How had I gotten here?

How would I get myself out of this mess?

I wasn't happy.

I didn't feel that I fit in this phenomenal place anymore.

Why didn't I feel like I did a month ago?

That was the moment he stepped in. It's odd how there are some people who have an uncanny sense of when they are needed and show up precisely at the right time.

David had this sixth sense. But he was not the usual boss. An introvert by nature, he leads by doing and show-ing and less by telling. I wanted to be his protege, and I thought that meant by doing what he was doing. What he was doing was staying late at work, which meant I was staying late at work. We both always stayed late to work. There was work to do, and I was trying to stay ahead while juggling work, life - which probably meant laundry and a cute little dog, and a demanding master's program.

As David rounded the corner mid-step, he asked something about how I was doing…

My response: "I'm not doing well" and then the tears began freely rolling down my face. I was feeling like a failure, but I still couldn't figure out why.

I was not a crier. And I never cry at work. But this time, with all the stress and unease of life, I was thoroughly spent and exhausted beyond words.

"You need to leave," David said. Mesmerized by his ability to read the situation, I was speechless.

He was kind, but these were not words of soft encouragement, but the advice I needed. David rarely gave words of sweet encouragement, he told you what you needed to hear. What would make you better, not what would make you happy.

Without judgment and with sincerity he told me I wasn't there yet. Not technical enough to be on the engineering side and lacking the experience to be a director. And to top it all off, there wasn't enough money in the budget for a promotion, that I desperately wanted and felt that I deserved.

My heart sank.

I loved this place, this job, and the people. This was my work home. This was the place I spent more waking hours than in any other place. Until that moment, I thought I would stay with this company forever, or at least until retirement, but that seemed like forever to a twenty-some-thing young professional. Working at a company for thirty years was a goal I had in my mind as what success looked like in Corporate America. My Dad had worked for the same company for many years and had no ideas of leaving. Those who I knew as successful career people didn't leave their companies. Success meant working through hard times and being diligent. No one I knew who was success-ful ever changed jobs. It was unheard of to me - but my knowledge of what success looked like was very limited.

But David was right. I needed to go; I felt it in my bones. I had worked myself into doing so much work to prove my value, but I couldn't continue to work like this, it wasn't healthy for the department or me. I often worked such long hours that there was no time for anything else in life other than work and the MBA program I was working on completing. And because I worked so much and kept so many tasks to myself, I didn't allow anyone else to share in the work. I hoarded work, not because I was power hungry, I just thought by doing it all, I was successful.

I loved working for David. His wisdom was awe-in-spiring. Often I was mesmerized by how he made decisions and enamored with his ability to think quickly on his feet. If I left, I would be leaving a great boss and no longer privy to working alongside a great thinker. The thought of leaving felt like I would be abandoning this great company.

There will be a day when you email me to ask me for some advice. Or he said something in that regard. That would be our new relationship. No longer boss and employee, but friends. Those words meant a lot to me. As a trusted person on his team, my role had been changed, and I had earned that change. I was leary of this change, but change nonetheless was needed.

That day, at that moment, **I lost the idea that I would work for the same company forever**. I lost the notion that life was perfect and fair, and success was staying in one company for your entire career. It was an idea that was shattered, but not in a way that was unkind or not true. David was kind enough to see my potential and the dangerous downward spiral I was taking if I didn't make a change.

Many years have passed since that conversation, and David's words have rung true. I often think about his words at the right time, telling me to leave. Without David's prodding I would have stayed and become resentful for what could have been when I didn't seek a new opportunity. His poignant words helped to guide my career to do jobs that sitting in that office with that large printer, printing budget reports never seemed possible. I am forever grateful to David for his words of wisdom. And I am glad that **I lost the idea that I would work for the same company forever.**

Donita M. Brown

Donita is proud to call Springfield, Tennessee home and shares it with her husband of almost twenty years, two beautiful daughters and a standard poodle. She's the creator of Wisdom From Others and enjoys helping others share their stories. When not writing, she is a professor at Lipscomb University teaching courses in Management and Healthcare in the College of Business. Often on the weekend you can find her either at a Bluegrass Festival where her daughters compete in many events, including clogging, square dancing, fiddle, and guitar or hiking on a quiet trail.

Finding Replacement Fuses

Robert Kannard

I'm pretty sure nobody likes talking about their childhood. It's so distant and alien-like you're talking about another era on a far-away world. For the majority of my life, my childhood was like a fuse box; I couldn't change how essential it was, but I prayed that I didn't have to peer inside.

I used to have six-inch-long sideburns (and I mean horizontally and vertically), I used to think chocolate milk was the be all end all of beverages. I used to be someone unrecognizable, and now I'm not. In day-to-day life, there's no reason to look back into that broken funhouse mirror.

That's not the only reason I leave the fuse box alone. If it were just style choices and an evident lack of wisdom, I could look into the box and laugh. Those little things would just be embarrassing mishaps that would age into funny factoids and then into pure, unadulterated nostalgia. The box doesn't just have peaceful memories.

I had a significant transition in May 2017. To keep things simple, we'll just say I moved out of one house and one household into another. I was no longer surrounded by the people who filled my little fuse box with broken fragments of hateful memories. Finally, I started anew.

I was numb for those first few months. My feet never really felt like they touched the ground. Somewhere, in the back of my mind, I knew of how monumental this change had been, but the full weight of that realization wasn't hitting me. I wasn't happy, or relieved, or sad, or angry, or anything. I was drifting.

For a while, I felt as though someone had told me the location of a giant door, behind which held all the answers. There, I'd make peace with the past, hold my head up, and truck forward into the future that so many people were telling me I'd have. I'd go up to the door, expecting it swings open with the sound of horns and the smell of roses, and it wouldn't budge.

That's not to say I expected all the dead fuses in my box to go away with the whisk of a magic wand. I wanted the door to open up to a place where I could begin the process of healing. I couldn't start where I was, even though I'd tried as hard as I could.

After months, I figured out what the problem was: the dead fuses were preventing me from opening the door.

There were so many things I didn't know how to do. I didn't know how to heal. I'd never done it before. That fuse was missing. I forced myself to dig a little deeper into the fuse box, into the foundation of my being, and I found fuses that were either burned out or never installed.

I wasn't sure where I could **find replacement fuses**. There is no hardware store of the soul. Even if I could track down the right parts, I wouldn't know how to put them in. That was another skill I was without.

For a long time, I felt like one of Rudolph's broken toys. I wanted to heal with everything in my being, but the healing wasn't coming. Once again, I was floating. I didn't have any walls to push off of or any ground below. It was just me, empty space, and a door that wouldn't budge.

I spent a year in this vicious cycle. I'd look into the fuse box, get frustrated, and launch into gray, empty space until it was time to come back down and look into it again. I was getting nowhere, and I knew it. I knew I was a story-teller. Character development comes to me as effortlessly as breathing does. This was the one story I couldn't write, the one character I couldn't analyze, and the one problem I couldn't wrap my head around.

The curious thing about fuses is that they can be tiny. The fuses in your car are so small that you could step on one and not even know until it's shooting pain into your foot. That pain is a message, a screamed warning that something unexpected has appeared in a place you wouldn't think to look for it. I didn't find my first fuse until it was yelling in my face.

I was sitting on a bench in downtown Nashville waiting on a bus in July 2018. It was a beautiful day out; large, fluffy clouds dominated the sky, couples walked along hand in hand, dogs sniffed the warm, wet summer air, and even in the busy, bustling city, my world was at peace.

Out of nowhere, I realized how beautiful this all was. The clouds were the most amazing things I'd ever seen. They were so intricate, with each rise and slope shaded by the sun. They weighed a thousand tons, and yet they were so delicate that the shapes would change with the wind and I'd never see a cloud like it again. They were just the way they were right then, and I bore witness to them. The couples passing by were oblivious, and for just a moment, I was a witness to their story. I'd likely never see these people again, and that's what made it even more special.

The first fuse I'd replaced was hope, and it was the most important one. A switch had flipped in my mind from that day forward. I noticed little synchronicities; numbers and symbols that spoke to me and told me I was on the right track. Some people would call them a coincidence, and some would call them divine. I don't really agree with either label, but from that day forward, a relationship between the universe and I had been cemented. That is undeniable.

Hope became wonder. I wrote a short video entitled "Wonderment" about my experience, telling my viewers that wonder comes from every tiny thing out there, from flowers and clouds to canyons and mountains to people in love and dogs sniffing the air. People loved that video. I had people I knew from before the significant shift tell me how different that video is from the person I was. It made some people cry.

What people don't know about "Wonderment" is that it's not just a hopeful message, or some ideal I try to live by: wonder is a means of survival for me. I've always been an optimistic idealist, but for so much of my life, it pushed me into a box that made me a miserable nihilist. Wonderment is a direct rejection of my past, and my life as it stands today would not be possible without it.

The world felt bright. For the first time in my life, I was doing well in school; I was making friends, and I knew where I wanted to go. For the first time in nearly 18 years, I was delighted with where I was. I was so satisfied that I was having trouble letting go of it. My high school graduation was right around the corner. After that passed, I wouldn't be able to go back to this place I felt safe in, with the people I felt safe around. Even if I did, it wouldn't be like it was.

It terrified me. I was scared beyond anything that these enjoyable strides I'd made would go away that I'd never feel that safe, loved, or fulfilled again. I was scared

I'd drift away just as I'd found something to latch onto. I had wonder, and I had hope, but there was a vast shadow blocking out the brightness of the sky.

I had another problem I had to overcome. This one wasn't a fuse; I couldn't just plug this in, like any old skill or realization, and make the problem go away. This was bigger than that. It was ultimately the reason **all the fuses had burnt out,** to begin with.

I had lost my childhood. For reasons I don't think I'm quite ready to go into and you probably don't want to hear, I grew up too fast. It wasn't one inciting incident or large scale trauma or anything quite that dramatic. It was years of being asked to step up to a plate I had no business being at. Years of worrying like an adult (for an adult) made me never really get to feel what it's like to be a kid. It overloaded my circuits and burned me out.

It wasn't like I could just become a kid again. I have stuff to do and a man to become. I was a month away from graduating from high school. I couldn't turn the clock back ten years, and I'm not sure it would really help if I did. I could finally mourn, and I had to make peace with it.

I did this at the happiest place on Earth.

I took a trip to Disney World in April 2019. It was a senior trip with a bunch of classmates, which made this event even more poetic. It was the third day of our three-day trip, and we had spent it in Magic Kingdom. We'd been to all four of the big parks, and I was feeling it. I rode my first roller coaster. I rode Tower of Terror and screamed so hard my voice went out for a few hours. I met one of my childhood heroes, and even though he's just a walking carpet with a crossbow, I had a good cry outside afterward. Say what you will about the mouse ruling the world, but I was having a good time.

That night, Disney had quite a show for us: fireworks display right above the castle. We'd gotten to Magic Kingdom around noon, and even after six hours of walking around the park, I wasn't quite over that castle. Walking up Main Street, USA and glimpsing it for the first time, I teared up. I'd seen pictures before, but nothing was like seeing it in person.

My best friend had insisted we get there three hours early, right as the mid-April sun wheeled its way towards setting. We sat on this tiny curb, right where the sidewalk splits in twain and curves towards the castle. It was a beautiful evening. Clouds dotted the orange sky in hues of purple. People insist the photos I took were edited and looking at them now, I almost wonder myself. There was magic in the air.

I'd felt magic radiating from places before. Right after I made the Wonderment video, I took a trip to New Orleans. The French Quarter had its own effects on me; the magic in that place was so strong it nearly overwhelmed me. It wasn't a bad feeling. It was unrefined and grittier, but as pleasant as anything I'd ever encountered. This was different. This was kinder magic, one that held and didn't smother, and it swept over me, unlike anything before it.

Right before the lights in Magic Kingdom began to come on, I noticed a cart stopped towards the castle. It was dripping with Disney merchandise; necklaces, little fans, and all manner of fare that kids would beg their parents for. I watched it for a few moments before making one of the single most fulfilling purchases of my life.

One of the items there was a bubble wand. It was in the shape of Mickey's wand from *Fantasia*, with a clear plastic mold of the aforementioned's head on the top. The top part lit up in every color you could imagine, and a steady stream of dime-sized bubbles spilled out of it. Something told me I needed to buy it. I wasn't sure what. Maybe it was the magic of this place, perhaps it was one of my shiny new fuses pointing me in the right direction, or perchance it was the promise of pure, dumb fun. All I knew is that I didn't care how much it cost, I needed one.

I walked up, timidly, and asked the lady running the cart for one. She told me how much it was, and I couldn't get the money out of my hand fast enough. Before I knew it, the wand was in my hand.

Here I was, a recently minted 18-year-old, who'd spent his childhood being afraid he wasn't enough of an adult, flicking the switch on his brand new bubble wand under the castle in Disney World. The bubbles came out, scattering out in a stream above the steady flow of people walking towards the castle. I moved it around, waving it in the air like I was trying to cast a spell. I twirled around in circles, dancing and giggling, watching the bubbles as they rose towards the sunset. My friends saw it too, and they were laughing right along with me. Tears started to gather in my eyes.

I felt free. I could laugh and cry over something so objectively silly. I wasn't freed from the pain, but I was free from suffering. I wasn't afraid. The most life-changing events I've had were moments: Wonderment, New Orleans, and now Disney came and went in flashes on a pan. Each one was a stepping stone to the next. Without Wonderment, New Orleans wouldn't have felt as unique. Without New Orleans, I wouldn't have been aware of the magic that lives in powerful places.

That door I'd be gazing up at cracked open. The way was paved, and I could heal. Disney allowed me to come to terms with the most considerable pain I carried with me: the time I felt I lost. I realized that I hadn't missed anything. The spirit of childhood is something we carry with us. I can see now that Wonderment was the first manifestation of that spirit crawling out from under the immense pain I brought with me. Disney tore down those walls. I will never again be without that childhood.

The other important revelation I gained from replacing my broken fuses is that there's a difference between pain and suffering. Pain teaches us. Because of the pain,

I held onto for so long, I will always value the wonder I find around me more than anything. My pain has given me that beautiful perspective. I didn't have that relationship with my pain before. My pain made me suffer, and suffering just hurts.

There's a child inside us all. Some of them are hurting, some of them are scared, but all of them are waiting for the chance to see the light of day and the wonder of the world. They don't have to wait for that next Disney trip to come out of the dark. Walk hand in hand with that scared little kid, and they'll show you how beautiful the world can be. Look inward, take a moment, and find them. Give them a hug. Hold them. They deserve it, and so do you.

ROBERT KANNARD

Robert is an Emmy-nominated writer and filmmaker. He enjoys consuming media almost as much as he does creating it. You'll often find him in a movie theater seat, with his nose in a book, or behind a camera. When he's not writing down a story (or listening to someone else's), he's making memories with his friends and family. Robert is currently attending the Nashville Film Institute's Cinema Production program

Mary Louise Morris

Missing Golden Opportunities

Mary Louise Morris

"You're a mother hen, Mary Lou." That's the words the Mom next door told me when I was a 15-year-old girl. That off-handed comment hardened my heart, and for many years I allowed it to keep me from grabbing an opportunity that was well within my reach.

Have you ever had clues, signals, and reasons at your fingertips to pounce on an opportunity, yet you allow that opportunity to slip away, never to come back? That may be ok if what you missed is something that comes around again, but when the opportunity is forever gone, then you come to realize that those little decisions we make in life are sometimes the most important decisions.

When I was a young teen-aged girl, around 15 or 16, I was a hundred miles different from many girls my age. Physically, I was less developed than most girls, and emotionally I was happy to be a homebody much more than a social butterfly who likes to have fun and lay in the sun.

Making things was my love. All I needed was a stack of how-to books, my sewing machine, and bits of paper, glitter, and fabric to make things, and I felt like I was in 7th heaven. I sewed clothes for myself and dresses for my mother and little sister. Being the middle child of a family of five kids, I had domestic responsibilities like helping to care of my little sister and cleaning bathrooms and vacuuming.

I was so much a homebody I gave myself a personal challenge one summer—to lay out in the sun on a chaise lounge for an hour each day and read a Nancy Drew mystery. I challenged myself because I neither enjoyed laying in the sun nor reading fiction books. Most girls my age would have considered that challenge ridiculously easy because they loved getting tans while passing hours away reading romance books, not that Nancy Drew was a romance novel. But you get my point. I know I must have been boring to many of my classmates who led much more worldly lives than me.

My childhood neighbor and friend, Wendy, who lived right next door to me was, at least in my simple way of thinking, the typical teenaged girl crazy about boys, loved riding around in cars with them, was huge into the high school social scene and didn't give a hoot about anything domestic. She was a beautiful girl with a vivacious smile who eventually became our high school's homecoming queen. Wendy and I were the same age, but because of our birthday months, she was a year behind me in school.

One day around the tender age of 15, I was outside in my parents' driveway and Wendy's mother, upon seeing me through her bedroom window, cracked the window open to say something to me. She said, "Mary Lou, you're just a mother hen." That took me back a bit, and I'm sure I didn't know what to say to her.

Why she said that to me, I'm not sure, except I knew I was not like her daughter, nothing like a typical girl my age. And she sometimes didn't filter her words. That label left me feeling silly and insignificant. And being that she was an adult, and I was still a kid, I took her words to heart.

If the truth is known, I was just fine with being a "mother hen." I loved taking care of my little sister. No prouder sister could there have ever been than me. I loved pushing her in the stroller and taking her shopping, often finding myself carrying her in my arms on the way back home pushing the stroller that carried our packages. And I enjoyed spending hours at my sewing machine stitching garments and at the kitchen table putting together little works of art with paper, glue, glitter, and crayons.

While, I knew I didn't fit the normal mold for a teenage girl, the label of "mother hen" didn't sit well with me either.

Wendy and I were childhood friends from the age of 7 when her family and my family became neighbors in a new subdivision of cookie-cutter ranch houses. Wendy was the oldest child in her family of six, and I was the middle child in my family of seven. Since we lived directly next door to each other, Wendy and I spent much time together especially at her house in her basement where we madly colored in coloring books and played with our Barbies. One summer our friendship was such that we had matching shorts outfits—hers in pink to go with her birthstone color rose and mine in blue for aquamarine.

The elementary school years passed, and as Wendy, and I got older, we didn't hang out with each other nearly as much as we did as young girls. I guess you'd say we grew apart. Her interests and mine seemed to be moons apart. Wendy loved the social scene, and I loved the home scene.

But I blossomed in high school, and I found my one true love at 16 and a half. I should say that he found me and we married each other within a year of graduating from high school. Dave was in the Air Force, so we traveled across the United States for the next twenty years. I eventually got my college degree in computer science.

Wendy went on to nursing school after high school. She and I didn't stay in touch over the years although I

thought about her often and wondered how she was doing. We had made so many good memories as kids, that
I thought of her as part of the fabric of my growing-up
years. She moved away, got married, and worked as a reg-
istered nurse in prestigious hospitals. But sadly, I thought
of her in shallow terms as my mind always recalled the
social butterfly party kind of girl I believed her to be in
high school, values I didn't embrace. I am embarrassed to
say how poorly that reflects on me, but I admit this hoping
to share a life lesson.

The years went by, and little did I know of Wendy.
Forty-some years after graduating from high school, my
aunt Clara died, so Dave and I traveled from Tennessee
to Ohio to go to her funeral. While there, we visited our
hometown, the town where both of us lived much of
our childhood. As we did most times when we stopped
there, we drove past our childhood homes. Upon driving
down the street where I grew up, we slowly drove past my
parents' humble house. My parents had both passed, and
another family was living there, but I still could feel the
memories of home just by focusing on the windows of the
house and imagining the years I spent there.

To the left of my childhood home was Wendy's
childhood home, and I saw that a car was parked in the
driveway. I knew Wendy's father had passed years earlier,
but I wondered if her Mom was still there. So, on a whim,
we stopped and knocked on the door. I almost couldn't

believe it, but her Mom answered. Knowing she probably wouldn't recognize me right away, I began to explain that I was Mary Lou, the girl who lived next door. Wendy's best friend in elementary school.

To my heart's disappointment and surprise, I could tell that Wendy's Mom, who was now in her mid-80s, didn't remember me. How could she not remember all those years that my family and hers were neighbors? Should I have mentioned that I was the "mother hen" girl to jog her memory? But I realized it wasn't her fault that her memory of those years failed. However, she was kind and invited Dave and me to come inside.

Not much changed inside Wendy's house; the front room still looked simple as I remembered, yet older. There was a man whom I didn't recognize sitting on the couch. He introduced himself as Wendy's husband. Immediately I was very excited thinking Wendy must be visiting her Mom, and I would get to see her. What a serendipitous chance of fate! Just the fact that we even drove here and stopped by to see Wendy's Mom was awesome, but then to learn that my friend Wendy was here, too.

That excitement was short-lived because her husband told me that Wendy was in the bedroom napping and that she was in the later stages of cancer, recovering from her recent round of chemo. My heart sunk. It had been 40 years since we had seen each other. And now, she was only

20 or 30 feet away from me, yet I could not see her. It was a very odd, sullen moment for me.

Her Mom said that maybe Wendy would get up and I could see her, but Wendy kept napping. We awkwardly stayed for about half an hour, hoping Wendy would wake and come out, but she didn't. Or maybe I would be invited to go back to see her. But I wasn't. I never really knew if she realized that we were there. And if she did, would she have wanted to see me? Or was she too ill or too weak? I didn't know. Twice now, I would miss the opportunity. I missed it by not staying in touch because I felt that I was too different from her and then again; I missed it when she was too ill to see me.

Not having seen her for 40 some years and then unexpectedly visiting her Mom while Wendy was there was like a chance meeting without the meeting. With a heavy heart, we left and traveled back to Tennessee, where we lived.

Over the next few months, I thought a great deal about Wendy, how she was doing, where she was. The day I visited her childhood home didn't afford me the luxury to know any details of where she lived, nor the depth of her illness. It seemed inappropriate to ask her husband a lot of questions, and her Mom's memory was poor.

The story I had told myself for the past 40 years about Wendy being so very different from me had softened, and she became much more real to me as a person. Here she was, near the end of her life.

In the following days, weeks and months, I tried - but not hard enough - to get hold of her before she passed away. With all the tools and search engines on the internet, I bet I could have located information for reaching her, but I told myself that she probably didn't yearn to hear from me. I know now I was very wrong about that. The one day I got very serious about finding her contact information is the day I found her obituary, and I was very, very sad.

Her obituary told not only about Wendy having a loving husband, wonderful son and daughter but also about the many years she was a beloved nurse and how she then became a nursing teacher. It sounded like she had a great sense of humor and a very warm personality. I couldn't have been more wrong about the way I thought of Wendy over the years, and I will be the first to admit that.

Her obituary said, in part: "When the toll of her illness took Wendy away from the profession she loved, she continued helping others by donating the crochet skills she learned as a young girl from her grandmother to make prayer shawls for charity and enough blankets and scarves to keep her family warm for years to come. Never one to throw a pity party for herself, Wendy stayed positive throughout her illness and saw that everyone around her did the same."

I felt about two inches tall, thinking of how I didn't put enough effort in reaching her in her last few months on this earth. My small decision to not exhaust my resources to reach her, talk to her, send her a card or anything made a significant impact on my life. Another golden opportunity missed. I learned a hefty lesson that day.

I think in hindsight, that Wendy would have been delighted to have heard from me and that we would have had more in common with each other than not. I didn't know to take the opportunity to the woman who spent 40 years helping to heal people. The woman who cherished her Grandma's crochet lessons and made warm blankets and scarves for her family. The woman who was selfless and positive and giving. Missing out on those 40 adult years was indeed my loss. All because of the stories I told myself from childhood. But I can always treasure those years we played together as young kids in her basement and backyard.

I hope that we become more aware of our stories and question whether or not they hold water. Sometimes we hold on to stories to make us feel better about ourselves, but in doing that, we miss opportunities to love and cherish the people with whom we travel this journey of life. I hope you have the courage to question the stories about yourself and others to give yourself the power to love more and do more.

When we can do that, let go of those old stories that tarnish what's accurate, we will uncover opportunities in our personal and business lives. When we shut off people for whatever reason, we also shut off connections we could have made and golden opportunities to do things together.

I imagine the friendship Wendy and I could have had as adults and the things we had in common, but I missed a golden opportunity. I mourn the memories we could have shared with each other. I think of how I could have shared my internet skills with Wendy who crocheted prayer shawls and how far and wide we might have been able to reach. It may sound like a pie-in-the-sky idea, but in today's world, just about anything is possible.

Mary Louise Morris

I am married to my high school sweetheart and best friend. We have been blessed with a wonderful family that includes awesome grandchildren we love so much. I started writing to help kids understand that their thoughts shape their lives. I wish I had realized the importance of knowing that when I was a kid. So through my writing, I hope to impress upon kids the importance and value of being grateful and focusing on what is good. I wake up excited every day, always dreaming of great things the future holds. Be the best version of yourself and never give up. I am the author of the Molly Jo Daisy series of children's books on Amazon.

When a Gift Hits You on the Head, Open It!

Jennifer Rachels Dix

It was three months and three days after my fortieth birthday, and I was on the floor. I could not move, I was in pain, and I had to pee. I'd simply tried to get out of bed when something in my back seized up, holding me hostage in a hunched over position staring at the honey-colored hardwood. This would not do. It was 5:30 A.M. on Monday and I had places to be. *Maybe if I just had something to hold on to I could pull myself up to standing.*

I reached for the bookcase next to my bed. Easing myself up, still hunched over, my legs betrayed me, and I went down. Knee, hip, hand, all met the bedroom floor. Grabbing the bookcase turned out to be a bad idea. I saw Z: A Novel of Zelda Fitzgerald tumbling towards my face in slow motion before the sharp corner of Therese Anne Fowler's story of the Fitzgerald's and the Jazz Age struck my right cheekbone and thudded onto the floor next to my head.

So this was what the fourth decade of my life would be like, eh? They would find me sprawled on the floor amidst last night's laundry, a shiner from a book I kept meaning to read but hadn't gotten around to yet, unable to get up, still having to pee—if my bladder hadn't failed me by then— and wishing desperately for a Medical Alert bracelet.

The lesson, although I didn't grasp it was when a gift hits you on the head, open it! The Universe was handing me a gift, losing my "youth" was actually the gift of aging and a chance to grow older, experience things I hadn't yet, and to say yes more often. It was well past time for me to tear into the wrapping.

However, I wasn't ready for that just yet, and from my vantage point on the bedroom floor, my forties weren't going so well. I remember my parents in their thirties and how old I thought they were at that age, yet I'd handled turning thirty semi-well enough. But most of my thirty-ninth year was a study in dreaded anticipation of the big 4-0. A few years prior I'd started noticing some bodily aches and pains that I wasn't used to and had no time or patience for. No longer could I sit on the floor playing with my young daughter and get up quickly. My joints were stiffer in the morning, it took me longer to get going, and I was discovering more than a few gray hairs. I dreaded my fortieth birthday and tried to put it out of my mind.

I pleaded with my friends not to acknowledge the day and to become accomplices in my no-fail, the ingenious plan of pretending it wasn't happening. My retort to the line, "age is just a number" was "yeah, but forty is a huge number!" I had issues.

I believed I had to accomplish great things before time was up, and I was too old and frail to do anything active. So I went skydiving at thirty-nine as if that would be the last bucket list item I'd ever do. Young whippersnappers in their twenties kept looking at me funny, or so I imagined. A friend's daughter, half my age, had stared blankly at me when I mentioned my excitement over going to see Eric Clapton in concert, and even an off-key but mostly recognizable serenade of the chorus to "Layla" garnered nothing but a clueless shrug. So I muttered "get off my lawn" under my breath and took my lunchtime multivitamin. Looking back, I was dramatic, illogical, and my fifty-year-old self will have a field day reading about this in about seven years. Wait, what? FIFTY? Queue brand new panic attack.

One night after a couple of drinks, I journaled what felt like a million different fears about turning forty and aging. It was a laundry list of angst. On several pages of a leather-bound book, I'd written about my belief in the misnomer that everyone I knew forty had it all figured out, and I didn't, hence my anxiety and the feeling of being behind in some imaginary but significant race.

Forty seemed like the culmination of all my failed attempts of getting organized and figuring out my life. My body, my career, and my creative endeavors didn't look like I had thought they should by this time. I felt like I hadn't done enough things, been to enough places, or had enough experiences. I focused on what I hadn't done yet, rather than what I had accomplished. My mind was looking back instead of forward. I also hadn't conquered my depression, as if mental illness is something you "fix" like a scraped knee or a broken bone.

I worried too much about what people thought of me, I hadn't yet figured out how to come into my own and show the world my authentic self. Would I ever overcome the fear of being me? What does that even mean? And what do you call the space between a quarter-life crisis and a mid-life one, anyway? Where's a paper bag I can breathe into?

Can you blame me for being a little freaked out? Women, in particular, are bombarded with messages that aging is something to fight, rather than to embrace. We see it everywhere! In magazines, online, in every media channel—what not to wear once you turn forty, how to defy the natural process of aging by using lotions and potions on your face and body. Forty-before-forty bucket lists you'd better complete or else you were a failure, exercises, and gadgets to fight wrinkles, double chins, cellulite, and sagging skin, dieting tips for your aging body and slowing metabolism, how to wear your makeup appropriately as a woman of a certain age, and on and on and on. There is a handful of positive and upbeat "your forties are the greatest age ever" messages, too, but as a natural pessimist, I only internalized the negative ones. These thoughts weighed heavily on my mind as I lay on the floor next to Mrs. Fitzgerald, cheekbone throbbing and eye swelling.

My dear, sweet husband of two decades eventually walked into the room, helped me off the floor between fits of not-so-stifled laughter, and my life as a forty-something went on. Over the next couple of years, the anxiety about aging that I'd journaled about so ferociously abated and one by one, morphed into something different, unexpected, and most welcome. I was learning that when a gift hits you on the head, open it.

There wasn't just one thing that flipped the switch on my perspective. I don't believe that one's mindset is usually changed by a single action—you have a better shot of success by practicing multiple strategies and realizing that some work better than others and some don't work at all. Coming to terms with the loss of my twenties and thirties hasn't come overnight, and I realize that the second half of my life is meant to be a series of mini-lessons that build one on top of the other with a common theme of accepting and embracing the confidence and change that comes with age.

I think the transition began when I started seeing a therapist, Dr. B, for severe depression. Depression has walked by my side for the better part of my adult life but I never considered seeing a therapist until the darkness sat too heavy on my chest and I felt I couldn't breathe. Antidepressants had been a part of my regimen for many years, but therapy was a new strategy to add to my arsenal when I felt that life's stresses had become too much. I was lucky to connect with an excellent therapist who I trusted and felt comfortable with, and this poor, patient woman knows more tedium about me than ought to be allowed. We should all be able to open up to an objective, neutral person and share the darkest parts of us. She has witnessed me at my most vulnerable and my happiest and has coached me through emotions of self-loathing, apathy, and everything in between in ways I could never repay. It was Dr. B who encouraged me to explore meditation and mindfulness. I credit a regular meditative practice with playing a role in calming my anxiety about growing older and creating a space to simply be here now, at the moment. Without opening the gift of therapy, would I have found meditation, mindfulness, and other mental health tools? Maybe, but I'm doubtful. Those were unexpected and beautiful gifts.

Changes in my physical appearance were a massive part of my dread of forty-dom, not only the weight-related ones that haunted my younger years, but also new changes in my body that come with aging—aches and pains, the graying hair, etc. I'm not sure what I was thinking. It's not like you turn another year older and BAM, you instantly grow two heads on your birthday or something. But as a woman living in a society that teaches us that skinny is better than fat, toned is better than saggy, young is better than old, dyed is better than gray, smooth is better than wrinkled, and so on. It is difficult or almost impossible to possess a sturdy fortitude to maintain a sense of confidence as the years march onward and change you.

I can't remember exactly what led me to the so-called "body positivity" community, but somehow I stumbled upon it online and have soaked it in. Social media can be misused and damaging, yet also be such a positive and connecting medium. The key is knowing that you are in control of what your mind takes in. Body positivity taught me to simply click the unfollow button on any person or entity that made me feel guilt, shame, or unworthiness.

I made a choice to follow people who are living happy and full lives in the bodies they have now. It's taught me to recognize harmful messages in the media I used to take at face value and believed for years, and how to redirect my reactions and feelings to those messages. It's taught me that gray hair and wrinkles are a testament to the life you've lived. I've learned to open the gift of enjoying life in the present, not ten or twenty pounds from now.

I am enough.

I deserve to take up space, and I need not fit into a smaller pant size to feel worthy, loved, and darn awesome. There is so much to unpack around this topic, and I discover new resources and support in this realm every single day.

One of the things that gave me the greatest angst about getting older was that by now I felt I should have figured out what I want to be when I grow up. In my non-jaded and naive youth I had a plan. Get a business degree because that's nice and vague and you will have lots of options. I was right. It wasn't a wrong choice, practically speaking, but it was probably too practical for my capriciousness.

I always felt like life would be easier if I just knew what my "thing" was and I envied people who always seemed to have a clear direction. Like James from 7th grade who always wanted to be a lawyer and now he wears fancy suits with argyle socks and says strange words like prima facie and mens rea. *What was wrong with me?* I get bored and am ready to move on after a couple of years at most jobs? Why had I loved pursuing a liberal arts graduate degree as an adult and then inexplicably dropped out but now want to go back again?

My fickleness wears me out sometimes. But I've finally come to realize that my seeking, wandering nature and fearlessness in trying new things is a unique gift that has given me many fortuitous experiences and is how I've met many of the people who mean the most to me.

Who we surround ourselves with matters, and so many of my closest friends have been unexpected gifts. As an introvert, I keep my friend group small but create fierce and lasting connections with them. I feel like I'm developing the strongest friendships in my forties and building the tribe I want around me for the rest of my life. These are people, male and female, who I don't feel a need to present any false pretense about who I am. People who inspire me with their positivity, realness, and courage. I learn different lessons from them all the time. There are my musician friends who work multiple jobs to get in front of a crowd of five or five hundred and do what they love with no other reward than to leave it all on the stage. There's Casey, battling a rare form of cancer who will often say, "Jenn, I just feel like shit" when I ask how he's doing—I admire his bluntness about the struggle. I see myself reflected in my band of strong female friends with unique personalities, each bringing something different to my life and who I love for giving me a soft place to land and for loving messy, real, complicated, almost middle-aged me right back. These are my people, and I'm so happy to have found them.

The book that fell on my head that day? The bruise on my cheek prompted me to open it, and now I count Z: A Novel of Zelda Fitzgerald among one of my favorite novels. My forties aren't so bad now that I'm learning to accept the many gifts of aging, even if they come along with some new aches and pains. We are all some work in progress. I know I'm still working on living an authentic life while caring less about what people think of me and standing firmly on beliefs drawn from my own well and not someone else's. If the price I have to pay for the gift of loving myself with all my quirks is a head of gray hair, some extra pounds, and an achy back, count me in—I'm here for it. I'm certain that the next decades of my life, as many as the Universe grants me, will come with new lessons, more changes, and many more gifts to open. Bring it on. **When a gift hits you on the head, open it!**

JENNIFER RACHELS DIX

Jennifer Rachels Dix (Jenn) grew up in Palmersville, a small town in Northwest Tennessee. She has a Bachelor of Business Administration (BBA) with a concentration in Marketing from Austin Peay State University and promises to eventually finish her Master of Arts in Liberal Arts from Middle Tennessee State University. She has spent much of her career in market research and healthcare and has a passion for the non-profit world, specifically in the areas of homelessness and social justice. Jenn has been married to William for 20 years, and they currently live in Murfreesboro, TN, with their daughter and a few fish. A writer and creative at heart, Jenn has been published in Muscadine Lines: A Southern Anthology, and several local publications over the years.

I Am Both Stronger And Weaker Than I Knew

Kendra Kinnison

Twice, the lumps in my throat were so large that I almost couldn't speak. The first was opening up our Thursday leadership team meeting. Then, I had to pause before starting my report at our annual Owners' Meeting. After weeks of sharing near-daily updates, I couldn't get the words to come out.

I think it's because I'd finally realized that this isn't temporary. **I am both stronger and weaker than I knew** The life I had before the storm isn't an option anymore.

And that kinda stinks.

I liked my life.

I'm the General Manager of Port Royal Ocean Resort, located on a barrier island near Port Aransas, Texas. Our central pool area has nearly a million gallons of water flowing through 3 waterfalls and 4 slides. It's surrounded by 210 condominiums nestled against the Gulf of Mexico, and during peak season, our nearly 200 team members host thousands of families for their summer vacations.

It took a couple of hard years to figure things out after a complicated divorce and emptying nest, but I'd done it. I'd wrestled with the darkness and unfamiliarity, carefully crafting the details of a meaningful life.

Sunday, August 20, 2017, was a perfect example. I started the day with a 35-mile bike ride with two of my closest friends. I had fish tacos and a Topo Chico on the island before checking-in with the team on an essential facilities project. That evening, I sent the draft of the first section of my book to four early readers.

That was my life. Work was intense, but I'd found good rhythms. I swam in the mornings, took spin classes most nights, and enjoyed long weekend rides. I wrote nearly every day, and my book was taking shape. I visited my daughter and nephews on each of their birthdays and organized family gatherings on holidays. I saw my friends often and even caught a few movies at the theater. I'd booked a fall trip to Bangkok for an annual gathering of my favorite people.

And then it was gone.

On Tuesday, August 22, I went to bed praying that the Tropical Storm emerging from the Yucatan peninsula would dissipate.

On Wednesday, August 23, I made a decision that I prayed was wrong: we'd close and evacuate the resort at 11 am Thursday morning.

On Thursday, August 24, we initiated our Emergency Action Plan, and methodically executed our checklists. Five of us stayed.

On Friday, August 25, we made a second walk-through of all 210 units, ticked the final preparations off our list, and hunkered down as the winds of Hurricane Harvey knocked out electricity and, eventually, our connection to the outside world.

Making initial landfall as a Category 4 hurricane, Harvey came ashore with 130 mph winds and a 4-8 ft storm surge that damaged nearly every structure in its path. After regaining strength and moving towards Houston, the damage from Harvey would match Katrina as the costliest hurricanes on record.

On Saturday, August 26, we woke with the sunrise, began to assess the damage, and then worked through the next steps.

23 days later, I left the resort for the first time. For months after the recovery took all the energy and attention I had. It literally consumed my life.

And then something interesting happened …a friend asked if I wanted to join them on an Ironman 70.3 relay, running the half marathon portion.

Replying quickly, I said yes, with the irony striking me soon after. I'd swam and biked frequently, but I hadn't run in years. I had done no structured workouts in over two months. And I already had blisters from burning my feet on hot pavement.

On Sunday, October 29, (two months and 4 days after Harvey's landfall), I crossed the finish line of the Austin 70.3, even though nothing in my past showed that I should have. I hadn't trained, especially for hills. And the last race I'd trained for, I DNF'd, which means I did not finish. (Blisters, oddly enough.)

Something was different about me, and I knew it. But I couldn't quite describe it yet.

Thinking about this run, I told myself that it would be three hours of pain. And then it would be complete. I knew I could endure that.

We'd listened to the winds howl for over 10 hours, twisting metal, breaking windows, and hurling debris all around, during Harvey's landfall.

We'd managed several weeks with no utilities, entirely too excited to see the porta-potties arrive. I'd taken cold showers for the better part of two months, more than half of them in an outside trailer rigged up in the parking lot.

We'd navigated immediate triage, daily emergencies, remediation, insurance adjusters, communicating with worried owners, complete business disruption, refunding booked guests, coordinating contractors, and rallied our teams to provide thousands of hours of community service and launch a training program. The days were long and intense, but we stayed after it.

Since the storm, I'd slept alone on a mostly dark island with only the bare essentials and a security team posted on the perimeter of our 25 acres. I'd experienced swarming mosquitos, displaced snakes, flammable seagrass, cranky generators, extreme heat, and some frigid nights. My safety manager joked that it was like living in *Survivor*, *Naked & Afraid*, *Undercover Boss*, and *Hotel: Impossible*—all at the same time.

For three hours, I could tolerate anything. I'd just keep moving forward.

I now know that I can handle discomfort and uncertainty, maybe even thrive in it. **I am both stronger and weaker than I knew.**

When I gave myself the time and space to unpack my experiences and feelings from the aftermath of Hurricane Harvey, I had a lot to process. What I realized was that none of these lessons were new to me, but the nuances mattered more than I expected.

It's vital to have a solid foundation of health—sleep, exercise, and thoughtful meal planning. Fortunately, I'd spent the first third of the year updating mine, before Harvey hit. I even took a week off to attend Tony Robbins Unleash the Power Within, and ultimately chose not to go, but used the time to refocus my morning and evening routines—and wrote them down. I returned to that anchor after each major disruption. The core is simple: move at least 30 minutes a day, stay away from sugary drinks, and get to bed before 10pm.

For team challenges, I'm reminded that assessing and clarifying the situation is the leader's role—not solving the problem. This was uncomfortable at first, as I often felt vulnerable and weak. Eventually, I faced the scenario enough times to trust the process. If I can describe the gap and the context, someone will step up to fill it. Usually, they'll even have a better answer than I'd know was possible.

I've learned it's okay to have a hypothesis that turns out to be wrong. Curveballs are intense and intimidating, and we faced lots of them. Over time, we developed a rhythm of getting a potential solution on the table, then debating the options or adjustments. Or, recognizing when we were beyond our expertise and needed additional help.

In the first few days after the storm, I felt like I was wrong more often than not. I worried whether I'd lose the confidence of my team. It felt like every layer of new information, and expert advice contradicted our previous plan, and it did. After a few more roundtables, I realized that the core team appreciated the transparency and willingness to adapt to the changing situation.

It's hard to know when to take a break, and it's helpful to have accountability that forces them regularly. As a single woman with a grown daughter, I could go all-in when I needed to. That was an asset, and also a liability. My coaching clients provided the balance I needed.

I've been coaching for several years, through many personal twists and turns, but none as all-consuming as the first couple months of recovery. My initial thought was that I'd need to shut it down, but even that would take some explaining, so I started with just being transparent about the struggle. I soon realized that clients were learning through my experience and messaging them was helping me to pause and process. It also helped to think through their eyes and escape my current reality for a moment.

Most importantly, I have learned that **I am both stronger and weaker than I knew**. I can endure much more than I ever thought I could. Round one was a steep technical learning curve and integrating several team members into leadership roles. Round two was piercing darkness, primitive living conditions, swarming bugs, daily emergencies, and responsibility for reconciling the needs of several groups of folks. It was heavy, and I handled it.

KENDRA KINNISON

Kendra L. Kinnison, MBA, CPA, is the General Manager for Port Royal Ocean Resort and the author of Royal Resilience: Our Story of Surviving and Thriving After Hurricane Harvey. Taking a unique approach to crisis management, the resort's employees served over 17,000 hours in community organizations and participated in a comprehensive training program while the property was being repaired.

Kendra serves on the Board of Directors for the Texas Travel Industry Association, Visit Corpus Christi, NavyArmy Community Credit Union, the National Alumni Association of Texas A&M University – Corpus Christi, and the Advisory Board of the College of Business. She chairs the Texas BPW Foundation and is a Past State President of Texas Business Women. Over the last two decades, Kendra has served in leadership positions in a number of community service organizations.

Holding an MBA and BBA from Texas A&M University – Corpus Christi, Kendra is the youngest MBA graduate in the school's history. She is also a graduate of Leadership Corpus Christi Class XXX and was the Steering Committee Chair for Class XXXV. Kendra was an inaugural selection to Corpus Christi's Top 40 Under 40 list in 2006 and was a Y Women in Careers Honoree in 2005.

Losing the Mask

Rebecca Whitehead Munn

I grew up in a family of five girls, all close in age, born within an eight-year time frame. As I think about the young girl I was and the girl I am today, I see some similarities and some differences. The similarities are I am still loyal, practical, and driven. The differences are the face I show to the world now exudes my soulful passions and is my most authentic self yet, I look inward for acceptance, and I practice daily gratitude for the gray that fills in the cracks and crevices between the black and white of this thing called life. Through the profound loss of a marriage and my mother in my forties, I focused inward as everything I knew to be constant changed in my outer world. I birthed my own meaning of life and now live my life out loud, in an authentic way.

As a child, I learned to act in ways to please others, sometimes seeking approval and always trying to fit in.

My father was a higher education administrator, and I learned at a young age that I was to speak when I was spoken to, and otherwise look pretty. I admired him as he spoke with confidence and seemed to know everything. I would follow him around the house like a puppy and go with him on walks around the neighborhood, to be close and learn from him. As I did this, I honed a skill of focusing outward on what he expected of me and in the process created masks to wear. As each year passed, experiences led me to build more masks to coincide with my various roles, a daughter, a sister, or a friend, such as one time when I wanted to fit in with my older sisters. My mother made my older sister take me with her and her friends one day, not a popular request with my teenage sister who was spreading her own wings. I practiced what my father had taught me and spoke when I was spoken to and furthered the building of my mask. These masks represented the "should" view I had created in my mind based on expectations and beliefs of others, **little did I know, losing the masks of who I thought I should be, showed me who I was.**

My development up to this point had been grounded in my exposure to religion and faith-based concepts, starting when I was a young girl. I grew up attending Sunday school and going to weekly church services at First Presbyterian Church. As I entered middle school, I became very involved in the church, as I found it a welcoming and inviting place. I felt like I belonged there. I sang in the youth choir, went on snow-skiing trips, taught bible study, and went to summer camp at Mo-Ranch. I poured my heart and soul into everything I did with the church, building more masks as I focused outwardly. I was idealistic at this young age and thought everyone who attended church was like me, giving church and their faith their full attention. When I entered tenth grade, I started to notice that was not the case. This realization put a crack in the very foundation that had supported me, my faith foundation grounded in the church. I was a strong-willed young lady and a little stubborn and held a rigid belief that life was black and white. My discovery made me angry, and I started pulling away from my faith and church as I entered college.

My faith took a backseat as I navigated my college years. I entered college as a business major and planned to graduate with an accounting degree and attend law school, a plan that was my father's dream for me. I struggled through accounting and data processing in my sophomore year. After barely scraping by with a passing grade in my accounting class and ending the year with a 2.0 GPA, I started to question my major. This was a pivotal moment on the path to uncovering my true self, where the seed was planted in my mind that I might have a choice in the matter, of what I might want, what major I might choose if I really dug deep to uncover my passion. I thought about my classes and what I really enjoyed, then switched my major to marketing. My last two years seemed to flow more easily as I thrived and began to expand, excelling in school again. The notion of who I might be authentically started to take shape as I graduated and separated from my father's shadow.

As I started working and living on my own after college, supporting myself, I began to push more and more the edges of whom I was and set out to uncover what I wanted. My mother was a quiet leader in her own right. Her goal in raising my sisters and me seemed to be to empower us to believe that we could accomplish anything we desired. I started to notice my mother more and more with each holiday visit. I felt calm in her presence, and she somehow made me feel as if I was the only person who mattered when I spent time with her.

When I went home to my own apartment after spending time with her, memories started to flood my mind of the time I spent with her growing up, something that had been hidden from my conscious mind or stuffed away as I took her for granted. I started to remember how she always indulged all of my individual passions, including a memory of her sewing formal dresses for me after I would draw a style on a piece of paper in high school. As I lived in the shadow of my father growing up, I had not had much of a relationship with my mother. As I continued to reflect and question who I was, I uncovered a hidden gem—that my mother had empowered me to be who I wanted to be, affording me loving grace and support without boundaries. Following a snow-skiing accident over New Years of 1995, space was created for me to uncover and forge a relationship with my mother. I was able to feel her unconditional love for the first time as she acted as my nurse-maid in the hospital during my recovery from surgery. From that day forward, we both invested in building a loving relationship. This relationship enabled me to have confidence in myself and gave my heart a voice as I expanded, leading me on my path to living out loud as my authentic self.

I learned that as I transitioned through significant life changes—such as moving from Texas to California, away from my family, and choosing to get married—my heart began to expand more and I was able to consciously shift expectations I held of myself and start to joyfully accept life as it was. In the early years of my marriage, I allowed my husband's warm and caring sides start to melt the armor I had built around my heart. He had a charismatic personality and held expansive hopes and dreams for our life together and our future. I was drawn into his enticing world and allowed myself to follow his lead, losing a part of myself in the process. Under the surface of a well-put-together face I showed to the outside world, I started to feel a little conflicted inside, realizing I had silenced my voice and lived from a place of fear, straying from the place of faith I grew up in. I allowed him to make many of the decisions in our life and in a few short years, we bought our first house, had two children, added onto our house and bought a second home in the mountains. My husband was a passionate dreamer and continued to want more, but after spending my days working and nights taking care of our babies, I was starting to feel disconnected from him. I also noticed I had reverted back to the people-pleasing patterns I had adopted in my childhood. Following several job transitions as he struggled to find his place, I took on head-of-household responsibilities and we continued to grow apart.

When I faced the ending of my marriage and the terminal diagnosis of my mother, within a few months of each other, I entered a period of transformation as everything I knew to be constant in my outer life changed. With each heart-wrenching step of change, I started to dig deeper and further question the expectations I held of myself and started to consciously notice the various masks I was wearing. Hiding behind these masks inhibited my ability to live out loud as an authentic human, including my freedom of expression. As I walked the painful path of separating every part of our joined lives as a married couple, I was consciously aware that my two and four year old looked to me for guidance. As I fell apart inside, I needed to show a strong face to them. I dug deep and learned through trial and error how to take each day as it came, face the fear and uncertainty, and carry on. Some moments felt like quicksand, others like water, and every day felt like a wall of grief I had to face. Supported and armed with the unconditional love of my parents, I started each day feeling as if I were facing a mountain I was not able to climb and ended with breathing a sigh of relief that I had made it through another day. As I transitioned to our new home, I learned that my mother had been diagnosed with late-stage colon cancer. The little girl inside of me screamed at the awful timing of this news as I cherished our growing relationship and believed that her love gave me courage to uncover my most real self, one inch at a time.

My mother and I walked a two and a half year path together of her living with cancer as she endured treatments, celebrated a period of remission, and sadly accepted the metastasizing of her cancer, recognizing the resulting impact on numbering her days left on this earth. When my mother needed it most, I was grateful to have the chance to start giving more to her from my heart—something that had been historically hard for me to do, as I did not have a great deal of practice. Through my experiences growing up, I had built a protective armor around my heart, creating walls to protect me. Because I was a strong-willed girl and a black and white thinker, every time I had an experience that revealed something different than what I expected, fear grew in my soul. Over time, I chose to keep my heart protected, as I thought doing so would lessen disappointment. My logical mind believed my heart was safe and no one could stomp on it with this armor.

As I supported mother and listened to the voice of my heart, not my head, I was able to test out giving love in a selfless way to her, just as she had modeled for me. Over the next two years, I took many trips to Austin to spend time with her and continued the deepening of our relationship. During the same period, my roles at work changed twice. I was honing a muscle I didn't care for, adjusting to more change, and the only option I had was to surrender, go inward, and find strength. I added a daily meditation to give me space to quiet my mind and listen. As this practice continued, inch by inch my stubbornness and strong will started to soften, creating an opening for my heart to lead and guide me forward. My priorities seemed very simple at this point in my life—to be present in each moment and passionate about what I was doing, how I was feeling, versus achieving some feat, holding a fancy title at work, or conquering the world, all outwardly focused goals.

My perceptions began to shift as I deepened my faith through meditation and trusted my heart to lead my path. As signs of my mother's cancer spreading through her body grew more visible, limiting her days left on earth, I began dreaming of finding a symbol of connection once she had passed. I was in foreign territory, grasping for some way to maintain this deep connection as it had fortified my path to authenticity. I challenged my thinking and started believing things that my mind had not yet comprehended—such as trusting that there was more to life than what I had seen or could see. Through my experience of navigating a state to state move with my children and seemingly insurmountable agreement required from my ex-husband, I learned that if I was open to believing something was possible, then that something would manifest. Purple butterflies were one example. While I had never seen one in nature, I chose to believe they were real. And on the third day following my mother's death, I saw one in the park near my house. . Now, my changing beliefs about the purple butterflies have come to represent the arc of my personal evolution to living authentically, **losing the masks of who I thought I should be, showing me who I am.**

In the last fourteen years since my mother's death, I have honed my skill of accepting the reality each day brings, although that is easier some days than others. My daily practice of meditating now includes gratitude for my path as it unfolds. Trusting in the unknown has continued to teach me the richness life has to offer when I least expect it, such as countless experiences of encountering purple butterflies—in nature, on a card, or painted on a wall—connecting me to my mother. This past summer represented another dark period of going inward as significant life changes unfolded: I sold our home of fourteen

DONITA M. BROWN & OTHERS

years and downsized, we laid our thirteen-year-old choc-olate lab to rest, I launched my daughter and youngest child into the college world, and my role changed at work. I have felt my mother's hand in each transition as an active angel guiding my protection and encouraging me to go deeper. Once again as my outer world has shifted, I have chosen to surrender and continue to uncover more layers of my authentic self, day by day, step by step, honoring my own hopes and dreams in this dance called life.

Rebecca Whitehead Munn

Rebecca is passionate about rethinking possible and brings intellectual humility to all of her endeavors, including several teaching roles at the Master's level. Her goal is to inspire others to be courageous and learn about their loved ones' wishes, while creating life-long connections. Rebecca's award-winning debut memoir, The Gift of Goodbye: A Story of Agape Love, is her personal story of walking the End of Life path with her mother. Her second book, Demystifying the Cancer Experience: Stories from the Front Lines, is coming out September 1, 2020.

She is a healthcare change catalyst and value creator, having served in healthcare executive roles for several global companies. In Rebecca's 28+ years of leadership experience, she has achieved success with leading innovation of new business models, prototyping emergent community-based delivery models, and segmenting consumer delivery approaches yielding growth and client satisfaction.

She earned a B.B.A. in marketing with a minor in psychology from the McCombs School of Business at the University of Texas at Austin, an executive M.B.A. degree from the Leeds School of Business at the University of Colorado, in 2017, became a Nashville Healthcare Council Fellow, and became certified as an End of Life Doula in 2018. She is the Board Chair for The Hands On Nashville Board of Directors. In her spare time, she enjoys spending time outdoors with her two college-age children, friends, and family, practicing yoga, snow skiing, playing golf, and entertaining. She has lived in Nashville, Tennessee since 2005.

Love Never Ends

Linda Wilkinson

My father was a fiercely independent man. Born in Missouri in 1928, he was a product of The Great Depression. Son of an entrepreneurial immigrant, he grew up watching his father juggle the responsibilities of their corner cafe and his taxicab business. With that upbringing, my father had a great vision for the future, and a stubborn streak a mile wide. He was also blind.

As an eight-year-old boy, he contracted meningitis. Without available antibiotics at that time, he quickly became very sick. To the surprise of many, he survived the illness, but when the fever left him, so did his sight.

Nevertheless, he grew up, got an education, a job and moved away from home. Outside of Boston, Massachusetts, he raised his family: three daughters and a son. Into us, he poured his independence, his love of travel, and his indomitable spirit.

He wasn't always easy to live with. He had very strong opinions of the "right" way to do something and was very vocal when the task at hand diverted from his intended course.

As expected, his children grew to be independent and self-sufficient and began to settle away from home. My life path delivered me to Tennessee where I married and began to raise a family of my own.

The year before my father died had been very difficult for me. One of the most influential "teachers" in my life had died suddenly, leaving me feeling very lost and alone. Karen and I had been friends for several years despite living several states apart. She was many years older than I, and was to me a role model, a confidante, a voice of reason, and wise counsel as I faced the challenges of early adulthood, motherhood and marriage. Within a matter of days in early June, she became acutely ill, and died being worked up for a lung transplant. Following her death, I no longer had anyone to hold up the proverbial "mirror," gently stand beside me and say "look" - "This is the truth. This is the way". Gone was my reality check and my sounding board. Yet, in her absence, I was reminded, again and again, what she had told me: She loved me, and she'd always be with me.

Following her death, I muddled my way through my grief the best I could.

Now, a year later, my father had also died. From all accounts, it was a "welcome" death from his perspective. Over the years, my strongly independent father had become increasingly dependent on others for care and had reluctantly spent the two years prior to his death living in a nursing home. He experienced deep depression in regards to his dependency and living arrangements. Fortunately though, he was able to enjoy the anniversary celebration we held at my sister's house in Massachusetts. The day was spent with all of his favorite things: the outdoors, great food, conversation, and the presence of his wife, his four children, and nine grandchildren. The following day, my toddler twins and I returned to Tennessee.

Two days later, my mother called with the news. She had been asked that morning to come quickly to the nursing home where he resided. As she entered his room, he breathed his last breath.

After hearing the news, I did the only thing I knew to do. I wiped my tears and continued packing the diaper bag to take my little family to the gym. I quickly dropped the kids in the nursery, but instead of hitting the treadmill, I headed to the locker room. There would be no workout today. I needed some time and took solace in the quiet walls of the shower.

As I stood weeping in the shower, I realized how blessed I have been. I was overcome with a powerful blanket of peace. The trivialities of family life, gone, I considered my mother's question to me that morning: "Would you like to speak at your father's funeral?"

Hmmmm. I had no idea what I would say. I had never been to a funeral. But, as I stood there, water pouring down, I was showered with memories of things he had said to me growing up.

> *"Put things back where you found them."*
>
> *"Wash your hands after you eat"*
>
> *"This is how you use a screwdriver. And a saw. And a drill."*
>
> *"If you'd thought about it first, you wouldn't have to apologize now"*
>
> *"Don't be afraid to try new things."*

Suddenly, all the rules I had rolled my eyes at as a child, held great wisdom for me. Mentally, I began compiling the list of things I had learned from my father. They would become his eulogy.

> *I learned that there are other, perhaps better, ways to "see" than with your eyes.*
>
> *I learned that humor is a great way to address what the world perceives as your weakness.*
>
> *I learned that just because the world stares, doesn't mean you should not do it, or stop doing it.*

I learned that blindness is not the handicap; surrendering hope, ability, and perseverance to your 'difference' is; something my father often refused to do.

I learned the importance of "Attitude" and the consequences of both a positive and negative outlook on life.

I learned that the world isn't fair; how I handled the unfairness is what matters.

I learned that he wasn't always right.

I learned that I wasn't always right either.

It was in that moment, in the shower at the gym, I realized that my father loves me - present tense, **love never ends**. Though his body is no longer with us, the love that he gave through the years remains. His love lives in each of his children as we remember the lessons and utilize the skills that his loving instruction and guidance provided. His love lives on as we remember the days spent together at the lake and around the table. His love is carried forward as I raise my own children using his example. Like the love of our Heavenly Father, it is always present, and it never changes.

As I packed to return home to New England for the funeral, memories would trickle into my mind, one at a time, asking to be added to the list. Slowly but surely, I knew the words I would speak at his funeral.

I kissed my kids, leaving final instructions with their father for the time I would be away. Silently, I made my way to the airport, through security, and onto the airplane.

Once in my seat, as we lifted into the sky, I pressed my face against the cool glass of the airplane window and looked out over the darkening sky. I could almost hear my friend, Karen, laugh and say to me, "I TOLD you I would always love you." I smiled to myself and said, "yes, you did" quietly to myself.

As my siblings and I prepared for the ceremony itself, my younger sister and I made a deal: She would cry. I would speak. And so we did. All the wisdom that had been passed down to me through the example of his life, I shared with others.

Returning home to Tennessee, I realized within my finite human experience, I was beginning to understand the verse, "**Love Never Ends**." Both with my friend Karen and with my father, the love that began years ago will continue on in my life and into future generations. It will pass on to my children, and to their childrens' children. It will continue, uninterrupted, until the end of time. **Love never ends.**

LINDA WILKINSON

Linda was born and raised outside of Boston, Massachusetts, but has spent most of her adult life living in middle Tennessee. Professionally, she wears many hats including Nurse Practitioner, Nursing Educator, Massage Therapist and small business owner. She loves to spend time outdoors - preferably barefoot - and enjoys hanging out with her teenaged children. She has previously authored a blog - www.stalkedbygod.com, and published both short story and poetry.

The Crash Into My Life

Danielle Taylor

I heard screaming and smelled smoke. Everything was muted, and I couldn't move. With realization, the screaming was coming from me. The sound I was making was that of pure terror. There was a sound as someone came through my car speakerphone. I was sitting in the driver's seat pinned in place and unable to move.

"You've been in an accident, I'm here to help you."

A few moments earlier, I saw the car headed towards me and knew there was nothing I could do. At all. I guess the vehicle really hit me. I tried to open my door, but it wouldn't budge. Pinned in place by my airbag. There was activity outside my windows.

"Ma'am, are you okay?"

"I don't know."

"Was I hit?" I asked. I was still so confused.

"Yes, honey."

"Why did he hit me?" I asked.

"Baby, I don't know."

A lot was going on in those moments.

The day of the wreck I was coordinating a group at work for our annual service day. We were all meeting at the Ronald McDonald house to volunteer. Once back to the office I realized how behind the morning had made me, knowing that I would need to be at work late to catch up, I hopped in my car to grab a quick cup of coffee.

That's when the wreck happened. I make a point now to not refer to it as an accident. This was not an accident. **This was a crash into my life.** It is still the most prolonged moment of my life and the quickest moment of my life.

I have scars on my hand where I guess I tried to shield my face and instead broke my windshield. I still have a hard spot on my abdomen where the seatbelt saved my life. A space on my body I already have issues with, I have an area that has become hard and reminds me I am tough. I sat in the ER for hours. The longer I sat, the more uncomfortable I felt. My abdomen kept swelling and bruising wickedly from the belt and windshield.

Traveling to x-ray with blood dripping from my hands, I noticed my shirt still covered in glass. I would move as best as I could while the techs just kept apologizing. Even now, I remember just asking repeatedly:

"What happened?... I wasn't even on my phone."

I was so incredibly confused and so exhausted. The wreck both emotionally and physically drained me.

The man who wrecked into me wasn't drunk, that would have been easy. Instead, he was on a lot of drugs. Like A LOT OF DRUGS: Meth, horse tranquilizer, and more. The man tried to leave the hospital once he was cleared and marked "fine." However, my sister and I sat in the ER waiting, and as we waited, we had a third member of our party for a bit, a metro police officer. They assigned the officer to stay with us to find out the extent of my injuries to know what to charge the man with, as they held him at the hospital in detainment.

As more questions were asked, I only knew that I could not answer any more questions. The hospital also took my blood to make sure I also wasn't on anything or under the influence. In the coming months, I would be called to court and dismissed a few times. Learning that the man who hit me was on probation, had a revoked license, and no car insurance on the borrowed car he was driving added insult to injury. And made me incredibly sad for the life he was living.

The year 2018 was hard. I had just recovered from having my gallbladder removed. Leading up to surgery, I was living on a steady diet of daily smoothies and bland dinners. My skin had never looked better, and I had never ever wanted a cheeseburger and fries more. But the gallbladder attacks kept me from having what I wanted.

I was walking with a friend almost daily around the city. Living downtown was something I had always wanted to do, and we would wake up super early, meeting, and walking up to 5 miles. Physically I was proud of myself. I had never pushed my body harder or better.

I found a small studio that had become my oasis in my life. It was small and cozy and usually picked up enough to my liking. And while I had a summer taken from me, it has given me more.

At the start of the year, I had ended a long relationship, and I was getting to be Danielle and figure out what that means. Finally. Life changed after that day and the crash.

Relationships changed after the crash into my life. Evolving and showing me who was around and who just couldn't add me into their life in my altered state. From the man I was casually dating who showed up at the ER after I asked him not to. He didn't show up for me. Instead, he showed up to make himself feel better.

The older sister, who still feels like I'm her responsibility, was there almost before the EMT's wheeled me in and took me to her house afterward where she woke me every few hours because that's what you do with a concussion.

The friends who, while willing to brunch and talk trash about others, were uncomfortable with concussed me. Their texts became less and less.

And the friends who dug the hell in. Because family, blood or not, continue to show up. The weird thing about brain injury. You can sometimes feel the irrational taking over. You can feel the erratic play through. And you can almost taste the frustration of the missing words that are hiding under the tip of your tongue.

It had been a week to the day since the accident, and I was giving a tour at work. A consummate workaholic, I went back faster than I should have. And I stopped as I tried to think about the word I wanted to use.

"We can get you… the long power cord with the built-in outlets to use for laptops and electronics."

Later I realized I was trying to say power strip.

A day later I was on the phone with a friend coming to visit me. I was explaining where I live.

"At the front door, there will be…. A silver box with names alphabetically in it."

I couldn't think of the world directory that I can use to buzz people in.

Brain Injury. It's a scary thing. Like, point-blank, it's creepy. Mine presented in headaches, memory issues, moods, and language difficulty. And then I learned what concussion headaches mean. Feeling a dull pain start and before you know it you're just in substantial pain. Similar but not the same as migraine headaches. Both painful and stupid. It meant looking at my computer at work and after less than 5 minutes crying alone at my desk, because I never let the people who work with me see me cry, and finding something else to do while it subsides enough for another 5-minute jaunt to headache town.

I found dishes to wash, sometimes in the dark, closets to organize, pens, and markers to check in-between times. I couldn't escape anymore. I used to hop in my car, man I loved that car, it was an extension of me and my need for independence. That's the thing many people who knew me commented on when they heard about the wreck.

Up to that point, it was the nicest car I have ever owned, fully loaded, and month by monthly payment, a little more mine. I would take long ways around, never minding traffic really, listening to books and musicals driving to a great trail somewhere when I needed to escape.

Now that outlet was gone.

But I discovered I could paint. I had watched watercolor tutorials on YouTube and Instagram a month previously.

And one day when I was sitting at home, not able to look at my phone, not able to watch TV or listen to the people talking, not ready to go for a hard hike to knock my head on straight, I looked at my desk, and there was a pan of watercolors and paper. I was tired of wallowing in pain. If I would hurt, I might as well do something else while I played through the pain so to speak. I refreshed my "up-cycled" salsa jar turned painting water glass and sat down. And as the water and paint made valleys and ebbs on the page, my head didn't hurt anymore.

And after a few minutes of playing in the paint, my head eased up. Finally.

And after I finished a page. I could really sleep.

I decided to not immediately get another car. Number one, cost, and two, it freaked me the hell out. When riding with my father the first time downtown after the wreck, I about hit the floor of the car, ducking for perceived oncoming traffic no less than 10 times. And our lovely Nashville roundabouts, I would break into a sweat just thinking about riding with someone around them.

I went 6 months car-less, walking to work, riding with friends, taking Lyft, and saying no to things I literally couldn't navigate to. I now have a jeep that is a tank, no bells, and whistles - minus the backup camera and Bluetooth because... I'm not a peasant.

And I drive. A lot. Because if I'm in another wreck, first, wouldn't that be terrible but also, I don't want to have it happen to me as a bystander. And while I know, I wouldn't be able to stop someone else crashing into me. I don't want to be a passenger, helplessly watching.

And that's how I live my life, finally. *I feel like I'm in the driver's seat for now.*

Before the wreck, I was living my life, brunching with friends, tied to my socials (still am) and making sure everything was carefully cultivated that I put into the universe.

Now I sell paintings, I have co-authored a book and am working on another. The wreck may have taken that summer and a good part of 2018 from me, but now life is messier, more creative, and more mine. It's not perfect, it wasn't before, but it's mine.

DANIELLE TAYLOR

Danielle is is a middle Tennessee native. Currently, she lives in downtown Nashville and loves being a guide to coffee shops and new areas of interest. When not working, you can find her painting at a local coffee shop, spending time with her nieces, and finding a well-loved trail. This is her second time to work on a book with her favorite older sister. You can find her on Instagram @danitaylor615.

Loss Finds Us All

Jane T. Floyd

Loss finds us all, but loss found me early. His face first appeared in Lawrenceburg, a small, southern town in Tennessee when I was eight. Until that sad time, I spent my days surrounded by a large, close-knit family whose love was boundless. Along with many aunts, uncles, and cousins, both sets of my grandparents lived nearby. On Sunday afternoons our families would gather at my grandfather's home after church for dinner and singing. My grandfather taught shape-note singing and music filled our lives. So, on those lovely days, my Dad, Douglas, his three brothers, and my grandfather would sing hymns all afternoon. I can still hear their lilting voices singing "At the Cross" or "Just As I Am." As the afternoon moved into evening, everyone would join them in harmony.

My mother, Opal, taught school in nearby Summertown. She relished helping her fifth-graders learn arithmetic. I also attended school there for first and second grades. My days in summer were carefree, and in such a small community during the early fifties, even young children had a sense of freedom not felt today. At seven, I would walk a mile or so to our local library, select a book, and curl up in an oversized chair to discover adventures and explore other worlds.

Neighbors never locked their doors. In this farming town, most folks did not concern themselves with the larger society but worked instead to provide for their families and care for each other. After World War II, peace and prosperity prevailed. Yet, **loss eventually finds us all**.

In the fall of 1953, I enrolled in the local school closer to home for the third grade. My mother decided not to teach that year because soon there would be an addition to our little family. Walking to school each day, making new friends, and taking piano lessons filled my days. Life was good.

On January 1st, 1954, my mother went to the hospital to give birth. My sister, Dianne, thrived, but my mother at 35 did not. In the early afternoon of January 4th, one of my Dad's friends knocked on my teacher, Mrs. Alford's, classroom door. He took me to the hospital, but I did not ask why. He led me into my mother's hospital room. There, I saw my mother lying so still in bed, wrapped in her pink, chenille bathrobe. Two of the hospital staff moved her body onto a stretcher and took her away. My Dad,

MawMaw, and Pawpaw sobbed. I had never seen them cry. My mother's death shattered my calm, safe world. I sat by daddy at her funeral and held his hand as he wept continually. I tried to comfort him, but it wasn't enough. At the end of the service, they moved her to the vestibule of the church for one last viewing. Someone held me over the casket and told me to kiss my mother good-bye. I still remember the coldness of her face. I suffered nightmares for days after. At 74, I always remember the fear.

Loss finds us all. He sleeps under the bed and sneaks into the cracks when we least expect to see him. Neither hiding place nor safety zone will protect us. Loss of loved ones, loss of dreams, or loss of our firmly held ideas forces us to confront a life much different from the days we had expected. We must move through those loses to find new hope and new dreams. We may want to forget about the losses. But, in my experience, loss must be faced — and felt — until healing brings peace.

Yet, along with deep pain, loss also comes with gifts. From loss, I have learned the gift of compassion for others' suffering and a richer appreciation for life. Loss offers an experience — a life lived with awareness, observation, and honesty. Profound loss demands that one live a deeper life rather than one that skims the surface. Loss forever changes your path, but the gifts of loss can guide your steps along the way.

My Mom and Dad were especially close to his sister and her husband, my Aunt Agnes, and Uncle Albert. Before the age of six, my aunt took care of me while my mother worked. Every day when the day's work had ended, my parents would come to their house where Aunt Agnes had prepared a tasty feast for supper. It felt like I had two sets of parents to love me. When I was six, they moved to Illinois, and I missed them terribly.

So, there was little surprise when soon after my mother's death, they moved from Illinois to Lawrenceburg to live with us and offer love and stability in a time of family shock and grief. Their nurturing sustained me, and home felt like home again. As the days passed, I began to adjust to life without my mother. My Dad worked out of town, and his loneliness when he returned on weekends was palpable. We spent lots of time together, which I loved, going to the movies and singing songs. But, without my mother, he was lost.

Life moves on, and in time, daddy remarried. Then, I had a new family including a brother and sister. In the beginning, it was exciting. We moved to a different town, and all seemed well. But, blending two families can be challenging. And, ours proved just such a challenge that continued for many years. I swiftly learned that I had not only lost my mother, but I also had lost the family that was familiar. This new family felt so foreign, and I was not a natural fit. Yes, it is true. Loss in some form always knows where we live. **Loss finds us all.**

We moved twice more and settled in Columbia when I started sixth grade. I felt like a stranger in my home. Although my Dad still was attentive, something distracted him. And my step-mother seemed to resent me. So, I looked elsewhere for validation and self-worth and found it by being a good student. I loved school and excelled. At first, I thought I had managed my loss, but now I realize I was just playing a role to survive.

Then, in September 1960, a knock on our front door in the middle of the night again changed my life. I was 15 when loss called my name once more. My Uncle Coy, my Dad's brother, said that my wonderful daddy had been killed in a traffic accident. My step-mother's screams pierced the stillness. I could scarcely breathe. Sometimes, if not always, shock brings a cushion to numb the crushing pain that comes with sudden death. We went to the funeral home the next day for the viewing. He didn't have his glasses, and I was inconsolable until someone placed them on his face. This loss consumed me at the time and continued to overwhelm me for many years. This time, I buried my feelings and didn't try to find the courage to move forward.

This was a loss I could not pretend to accept, and I wandered aimlessly for so long. I felt abandoned and seethed with anger, mostly at God. "Really, God? You would take both of my parents?" I wondered. I started to smoke cigarettes and lost interest in school. My grades suffered. Without my Dad, the school held little importance. However, I survived and moved to Nashville when I was 18, although emotionally, I was probably only about 14. This happens when children have no support to deal with loss. When there has been no counseling or guidance, confusion, and aimlessness abound.

Life in Nashville gave me a freedom I had not experienced before. There, no one knew my name or my family history. Even with the trepidation of another loss as my constant companion, each day dawned with infinite possibilities. A new job, new friends, and cute boys consumed my thoughts. But, lurking below, unresolved grief tugged at my heart and never left my side. At 20 I met a special boy, and six weeks later we married. My desperation for security would be quelled, and I would finally be safe and not alone, eventually finding a family. The next twelve years brought us three healthy, happy boys and some sweet times. But, even though we did our best, the marriage died.

Despite mistakes, poor choices, and wrong turns, I met each day with determination. After my marriage ended in divorce, I sought counseling to help me understand my confusion and fear. It wasn't until I was 34 that I faced the truth that I needed help — so much help. My gifted counselor, Judy, taught me how to assume responsibility for my actions and claim my life. On my first visit, my three young sons and I sat on the couch. At this initial visit, my most pressing concern was to help my boys deal with their sadness about the divorce. Proudly, I told Judy about all the parenting books I had studied and tried to convince both of us I was at the top of my game. Nothing could have been further from the truth.

After a few sessions, I had many questions and few answers. It took a long time. But, with Judy's insight and my hard work and perseverance, I learned how to heal. I walked and am still walking on the path to becoming whole. I learned to forgive my parents for leaving me alone. At 48, I was finally ready to say good-bye to my daddy. So, I took a long walk and wrote a poem. I am no grand poet. Though, sometimes, composing poems* helps light the path forward.

One of the most treasured gifts after losing my parents was the surprise discovery of their letters. In 2002, 42 years after my Dad died, my stepmother passed away. Their letters were tucked safely away in a Sheffield Inn candy box in the attic. Some notes were those my parents had written to each before they married. But, most of them were ones my father had written to my mother when he was a World War II prisoner of war in Germany In 1944.

That these letters survived seemed like a miracle. Now, my sister and I could know our parents from their own words. We could hear them speak to each other when their world was young, and all things seemed possible. Mother was 26. Daddy was 20. Loss often comes with surprise gifts such as these.

With counseling, journaling, practice, and time, I realized that the losses in my life have strengthened me. Now, I have a sense of peace with my loss. I treasure the sweetness and joy of my parents' love as I strive to live each day in gratitude from the gifts of loss instead of the sadness of loss.

*Farewell to my Dad

The grave digger buried you.
And, so I buried me.
Sleeping restfully below,
Your face I could not see.

Except those times I closed my eyes
To sleep my restless sleep.
When spinning, dancing in my dreams
Came a ghost not mine to keep.

Oh, you went away and left me,
And, I knew not what to do.
So, I clutched my pain inside my heart
Instead of clutching you.

Now, it's time to say farewell.

The grief must know the tears.

The girl who joined you in the grave

Must look and face her fears.

That child must turn the tarnished knob,

Walk through that dusty room,

To find the cloak of love that waits

To raise her from the tomb.

From that frozen space and time,

From the frigid cold of night,

Slowly moving toward the dawn,

To walk with wonder toward the light.

*For Judy —My Amazing Counselor

I thank you, Judy
For the skills you use.
For choosing to listen,
For hearing my clues.

For seeing behind my
Games and my walls-
For leading me through
My dark, dreaded halls.

For touching and caring
And giving me space.
To sort out the devils
That cover my face.

For planting a seed-
For letting it be-
For watching and waiting-
Then, setting me free.

JANE T. FLOYD

My name is Jane Floyd. My husband and I live on top of a mountain in a small community called Shady Valley in northeast, TN. In 2007 I retired after 34 years with AT&T. I have 3 sons and 4 wonderful grandchildren. I enjoy spending time in the kitchen and feeding others at my table as well as reading and exploring new ideas and learning from others.

Letting Go

Lauren C. Dean

Daniel and I are high school sweethearts. We didn't go to the same high school, though. We went to rival schools just a few miles apart, but we were inseparable from the beginning. About a month before I graduated, Daniel proposed, and we began planning our future. We wanted at least three children, maybe four. All the little ones would have blue eyes like us, and all our girls would have my curly blonde hair. We laughed because our kids would be giants! We are both almost six feet tall after all.

Not long after we were engaged, we were told that Daniel may have trouble fathering children. Apparently, there was a botched surgery when he was very young, but no one could be sure how it would fully affect him at 20 years old. After some initial testing, we found that his counts were very low, and we would probably need some fertility treatments to have a family. As 18- and

DONITA M. BROWN & OTHERS

20-year-olds I don't think we grasped the seriousness of his infertility.

Fast forward four years, and I began thinking all was not right with me, either. Should menstrual cramps hurt *this bad?* Is it normal to actually *fear* "that time of the month" because you know what is coming? I didn't think so, and my doctor confirmed it. I had a huge endometriomal cyst on my ovary, and endometriosis was growing pretty much everywhere in my abdomen. That summer, I had the first of three surgeries to remove the cysts and endometriosis. It just kept coming back. I started getting shots every six weeks to slow the growth, and that worked for a couple more years until those injections began making me sick.

Meanwhile, Daniel and I went to a fertility clinic to see what we would need to do to conceive. Daniel's counts had dropped to almost nothing, and when I say almost nothing, I mean six live sperm were found. Six! Not six million or six thousand. Just six. That's okay, we thought. We would need to start the most extensive IVF procedures, but we were willing to do whatever it takes. Until... we couldn't get financing for the procedures. Bomb. Now it's hitting us. This will not be quick. It will not be easy. And how in the world will we ever afford it? We had Daniel's sperm frozen and said, we'll figure it out.

A year later, we got a letter in the mail letting us know that the yearly fee to keep his sperm frozen was due. It was hundreds of dollars. My injections were making me ill, and I had been discussing other options with my doctor. I can remember this moment so vividly. We were at a crossroads. We had to decide about our future— our family, right now. Standing in the kitchen, we talked about wanting children. That's all we wanted. Do we really need a child that looks like us? Can we afford to try IVF again if it doesn't work the first time? We knew the odds, and they weren't good. If we spent $14,000 on fertility procedures and they didn't work, how in the world could we afford to do anything else? We held each other and cried. **And we let it go**.

We let go of the dream of those giant kids with blue eyes, and our daughters with curly blonde hair. *I* let go of the thought of ever being pregnant, and I'll tell you, to this day almost 10 years later, that's the hardest pill to swallow. We decided it *didn't matter* that our children wouldn't have our genetics. We just wanted to be parents. That day was the beginning of our journey into adoption. Many people don't realize there is a loss in adoption. The birth parents have experienced the loss of their child, adoptive children lose biological family members, and adoptive parents have experienced the loss of their ability to conceive.

That summer, at 26 years old, I *voluntarily* had a hysterectomy. I was done with the injections, the surgeries, and the pain. What good was it to me, anyway? We knew our path. I will never regret that decision. It was the best thing I've ever done, and I could finally *let go of* this dream that somehow, someway a miracle would happen and I would get pregnant. I felt free. **For the first time, I realized that letting go of how I thought life should be would help me heal.**

We began researching adoption immediately, but we still couldn't afford to really do anything through an agency. We tried fostering. Maybe, just maybe we could adopt through foster care. So, we began the foster care classes locally. We completed every requirement except the CPR and first aid class when I got a phone call from a social worker. 'We're sorry, but unless you are willing to take a child 9 years old or older, we just don't have a need for you in your area'. Another crushing blow.

Around this same time; however, I found a small adoption agency in Nashville, and it looked like we might just be able to afford them. In September 2011, we got a letter in the mail from them letting us know that they were starting a new adoption class— one of only two they do each year. This was it. We were actually moving forward. In these classes, we discovered a tiny community of about 6 couples just like us. People who wanted to be parents, but couldn't conceive. Women who knew the pain and jealousies I felt at never being pregnant. We met the kindest, sweetest social workers, who really cared about all of us. People don't tell you what a long process adoption can be. We started those classes in September and were home study approved the next March.

Hopeful adoptive parents live in limbo during the long home study and wait. Our friends and family knew of our intentions to adopt, but it's typically not a celebratory time. There were no words of congratulations during the process, no well wishes from strangers in public, and indeed *no baby showers.*

We had a nursery set up from our attempt at fostering, and often I found myself in the baby room, sitting in the rocking chair, praying that God would fill that room with a child. I watched friends and co-workers conceive and give birth in those months, not knowing if we would ever be blessed with a family of our own. Often during the wait, jealousy filled my heart. Those months were a dark time for me, filled with fear and anxiety. I had no idea that God was working in secret and laying His plans.

On May 25, just over two months since they had approved our home study, I was getting ready to meet Daniel for lunch when I got a call from the agency. When I saw the agency name on the caller ID, my heart literally stopped, and I remember thinking, 'This better not be some recorded message!' It wasn't. It was our caseworker. A baby girl had been born a week earlier, and they had chosen us to *meet* with the birth parents. She gave me all the details and asked if we wanted to move forward, but stressed that it was just a meeting to see if it felt right. On

May 31, we met Melissa and Philip for the first time. I can't explain how four people who are so different can seem so much alike. We had met with two previous birth families, but this felt so different. After the meeting at Melissa's mother's home, we got back in the car with the caseworkers, and one of them said, 'They want to proceed with you guys.' I remember thinking, 'Say that again' in disbelief. Daniel and I clutched hands in the back seat. Philip and Melissa still had four days to change their minds, but as of the moment, we would bring our daughter home in the next few days.

The next day, on June 1, I was at a teacher in-service. I remember getting in my car around 11 a.m. and seeing yet another call from the adoption agency. In my heart of hearts, I just knew they were calling to say that the birth parents had changed their minds. To my absolute relief and surprise, they were actually calling to tell us that the baby girl was unexpectedly getting out of the hospital that day, and they wanted to see if we could bring her home! Um, what?? After calling and talking to Daniel, we went against everything we had promised ourselves about not bringing a child home before the parental rights are wholly terminated, and we said, 'Of course!'

On that day, at around 2 P.M., we met, held, and brought home our daughter, Elle. You know the saying, 'always a bridesmaid, never a bride'? Well, I coined the phrase, 'always an aunt, never a mother.' I remember just being in complete shock that she was ours. How can we go from wanting and praying for a child two days ago, and here she is? I was the fun aunt, the one who wanted kids so badly that I took my nieces and nephews everywhere so that in my mind I could *pretend* I was a Mom for a little while.

From the moment we met and held her at the agency, all the fear, all the anxieties, all the *jealousies* melted away. How could I have known that for the past nine months while I had cried, and prayed, and worried over ever being a parent, our daughter was being carried and nurtured and loved by her birth parents. God had a plan. He had a plan for all of us we couldn't see, but in His wisdom, He laid out our path. What a humbling experience to know that you have been chosen by birth parents and entrusted with their most precious being. I can't understand their pain, but I can only imagine the strength it takes to give a part of yourself away freely. I believe that's a strength that most of us will never be capable of.

We knew that they wanted an open adoption, and we were also receptive to that idea even though we didn't know what that meant for us yet. In our gratitude, we set out to honor the pledge we made for open adoption. It has not always been easy. The first time we met with Philip and Melissa after we brought Elle home was about six months later. For days leading up to the meeting, I had a lot of anxiety. I felt that Elle and Melissa would have a bond that I never could have. To my surprise, there was no 'magic' connection. Of course, Elle didn't remember them (she was a six-month-old!), and at the end of the meeting, she wanted to go home with Mama and Daddy. So, for all the anxiety I had beforehand, I felt at peace afterward.

Now, our open adoption is about so much more than gratitude. We want our child to know that she is loved by so many people. So incredibly loved. She has met grandmothers, an aunt, and her greatest excitement, siblings. Elle has two half-sisters and a half-brother, and open adoption has brought them together.

Daniel and I are passionate about open adoption because we continue to see firsthand how important it has been for Elle. She too has experienced loss. During the first meeting with two of her siblings, Daniel and I realized how much she is missing. She has three half-siblings who live with two different families. My first thoughts were, 'It's not fair that they can't be together every day. Siblings are supposed to be together!' But that isn't our reality. Once again, we had to let go of what we thought life should be and embrace God's blessings. We know that she misses her brother and sisters; she talks about them almost daily. But, open adoption has given them a relationship. While they can't be together every day, they also won't entirely be apart.

Through our journey, we have learned that adoption is a God thing. We have to let go of past pain to accept the blessings He has for us. I often think about the perfect timing that brought Elle into our lives. If we had held on to the past hopes of having biological children, we would never have been able to embrace the life God planned for our family. Our loss brought us our greatest joy. I've often said, life gave us lemons, and she's our strawberry lemonade. We would not change a single thing about our journey. Having our daughter, this tiny brown-haired, blue-eyed marvel, has been worth it all.

LAUREN C. DEAN

Lauren was born and raised in middle Tennessee, and currently lives just north of Nashville with her husband, daughter, and two English Bulldogs. She is an elementary teacher who is passionate about books and teaching young children to read and write. When she isn't at school preparing lessons or reading books about reading, you'll most often find her engaging in a little retail therapy. You can find her at @ lardean1014

Conclusion

Donita M. Brown

Just like any season of life, every book must come to a close. I hope this book has provided you with a few tears, a few smiles, and a few heartwarming stories. The authors in this book are my friends; maybe they didn't start that way, but I am delighted to call them friends now.

In 2008, I started writing a book. Well, writing is a powerful word. I would say I had an idea about a book. Then I would write maybe twice a year. I thought more about writing than I actually wrote. Then my friend, Andrew Kerr, author of *The Humility Imperative*, told me he was writing a book. I was mesmerized. I had never told another soul I was writing a book, but at the moment shortly after he told me he was writing a book I uttered the words, "I'm writing a book, too," and his encouraging words helped me move from thinking about writing to publishing now my third book.

The first book I wrote, Wisdom From Others: Life Lessons From My Dad, was a sharing of the wisdom I had gained through being Ken's daughter. It was a badge that I had worn proudly throughout my life and didn't realize until I had my own children, just how extraordinary the wisdom I had received from my Dad had been. His being a great parent and taking the time while also being a provider was something worthy to share with others. And I felt that this wisdom must be shared, especially with other working parents.

Being a parent is worthy and significant, but it is also hard and at times, gut-wrenching. There is strength in sharing the wisdom I learned with others in hopes that it would inspire other parents to stay the course and realize the work they are doing as parents are vital, meaningful, and essential. What I found after writing this book was that often, I was told by those who had read the book ally with about wisdom they had learned from their family members.

My second book, Wisdom From Others: Life Lessons From Candy Cane Day, was a joy to write because I was able to write it with my sister, Danielle Taylor, who is not only a fantastic writer but also an outstanding watercolor artist. Writing a book with another person was more enjoyable because we shared in the creation of the book.

Using the idea of sharing wisdom and writing with others gave me the idea and hope to help others share their wisdom. In this book, I have been the curator of eleven other stories, each as unique as their authors.

My hope with this book and the other two books in the Wisdom From Others line of books is that you will find some lesson in the wisdom shared.

While this is the third book of my series, I hope it is not the last and will be collecting wisdom stories from others for future stories. If you have a story you would like to share, please send it to me at donitabrownauthor@ gmail.com.

If you picked up this book after the loss of a loved one, please read the Epilogue, from Johnny Trail, as it may help you find comfort in your loss.

Thank you for reading. And I hope you will leave a review on Amazon if you liked this book and pick up my other books.

Epilogue

Johnny Trail

As evidenced by the preceding vignettes, grief is not a "one size fits all" proposition. Each person navigates through their grief process in a different manner. All people who are touched by bereavement have a unique familiarity that further defines the relationship they had with the loss.

Sometimes people in western culture are ashamed to show the depth of their grief. The displaying of outward forms of anguish is a cultural consideration. Some cultural groups are willing to mourn outwardly while others hold in all their emotional turmoil. Suffice it to say, those seeking to help people who are mourning should let them know that there is no harm in displaying grief.

That having been said, sharing our grief experiences primes those who must walk the path we have already trodden. Each person will endure the loss of a significant person in their life. One fact that is missed by those trying to offer comfort is that people want to talk about their dead loved ones.

The experiences shared in this book offer the synergistic experience of therapy in many ways. It is therapeutic to the one who shares their story of grief. When we read stories that discuss people's grief experiences, we realize that there are many commonalities to the grieving process.

Contrary to what is thought, those who have endured loss want to talk about the person who is dead. In our misguided efforts to avoid causing pain, we have assumed that people suffering from bereavement do not want the deceased to be mentioned. This is a misconception by those attempting to help the one suffering from loss.

One method that is followed in working with people who experience grief is to have them journal about their experiences in the loss. This helps one to organize their thoughts and reflect in a concrete way on what they are experiencing. In writing about their bereavement, they get to tell others about the severity and nature of their loss.

Furthermore, even though the deceased is not physically with us, we are still in a relationship with them. As previously mentioned, we remember things about them. We remember phrases they would say, things they would do and the way they demonstrated love toward us. They live on in our minds. When we are at our lowest, we can reflect upon their words for comfort and strength.

Moreover, it is therapeutic to the one reading this treatise. Who better to get directions from than the one who has already traveled the road of bereavement and loss? We sometimes feel isolated and alone in our solemn walk of loss. Books such as this one remove the sense of loneliness and depression that can be felt when we experience grief.

Death is a commonality among all humankind. We are walking a road in loss and bereavement that has been well-traveled. To that end, those who have suffered through the death of a loved one can offer suggestions to help others mitigate their grief.

We learn from the essays that loss comes in many shapes and forms. Loss can include more than the physical death of a loved one. It can include the loss of a dream, the loss of a job, the loss of a home, or some other event where one experiences pain.

This is one of the stories that is sometimes overlooked in the book of Job, in the Bible. One understands the severe trauma associated with losing a child or children. We do not always reflect upon the loss of wealth, status, and health that he suffered. These are all modern concerns associated with grief. Loss can come in many forms and shapes.

The quality of the relationship that was shared with the deceased can also determine the duration and severity of the grief experienced at the time of the loved one's death. There is a difference between losing a close relative and losing a friend that one had just met. One can experience sadness over loss decades after the loved one passed—emotions that are just as powerful and real as when they were initially experienced.

Loss can also provide clarity. Through loss, we learn to value relationships more. I lost both of my parents in 2005 and suffered a traumatic, synergistic loss. That loss taught me that I needed to say things that were important to those close to me. Telling people about our love for them and how much they mean to us becomes important as we understand how precious and short time is.

Finally, those who are suffering from the death of a loved one might feel some guilt that they have lived and their loved one had died. Sometimes the survivor needs to be reassured that it is all right to continue with life. To that end, a therapeutic method might include developing a theme for moving forward in life.

The deceased who loved the living would want those who remain to move forward in life. One might ask, "How can I best memorialize the one who is deceased?" This can provide a powerful key for helping a person to move forward in the grieving process.

JOHNNY TRAIL

Dr. Johnny Trail has been married to his wife Jada for almost 23 years. They have three sons, Matthew, Nathan, and Noah. Johnny currently preaches for the Hillcrest church of Christ, in Springfield, TN and has been preaching for over 31 years. He is also a licensed marriage and family therapist with offices in Murfreesboro and Springfield, Tennessee. He is an instructor for the Nashville School of Preaching and Biblical Studies. Johnny also is an editor for THINK magazine and writes for Gospel Advocate.

About the Author

Donita Brown is a professor author, speaker, and coach based in Nashville, Tennessee. Whether in the classroom or in the written form, Brown teaches others how to make the right choices, rather than trying to do it all, and learn from others.

The Lipscomb University professor teaches a Master of Healthcare Administration Program and undergraduate management and leadership courses. She began her career at HCA Healthcare, a global company that she credits for showing her the similarities between healthcare and education in the respect that we all need both. Brown's expertise is healthcare innovation and she enjoys teaching others how to evaluate new technologies and trends. In terms of teaching the concepts and practical application of management, her goal is to plant seeds. Brown is a source of comfort inside and outside of the classroom as she gives her students structure, guidance, and everyday skills such as how to listen, lead, and be directed.

As an author, Brown, creator of the *Wisdom from Others* book series, believes that the best advice always comes from others. The idea for her story collection, which includes four books, came about when she realized that much of the advice she received that had once seemed irrelevant was actually useful. *Wisdom from Others: 9 Life Lessons From My Dad, Wisdom from Others: 7 Life Lessons from Candy Cane Day,* and the forthcoming *Wisdom from Others: Life Lessons from Loss* and *Wisdom From Others: Life Lessons From Great Bosses* encompass the author's desire to provide others with a platform to learn from their peers.

By allowing her readers to contribute to and shape her series, the author has demonstrated that strength lies in numbers. She has expanded her reach, sales, and ability to positively influence through collaboration. "The collection of stories I am currently working on came about after people read my first book and began presenting me with new ideas, which is the beauty of being receptive to feedback," she explains. From that process, she has assembled her next projects.

As a public speaker, Brown approaches her engagements in a conversational manner, discussing the challenges that we all face in everyday life and wisdom we can use to get through it. She speaks at faith-based organizations and corporations.

As a life coach, Brown works with working moms whose daily dilemmas she understands. "I have two daughters, a husband, and poodle so I know the challenges of wanting a career and to also be present for my family," she says. She coaches working moms on how to focus so their personal and professional lives flourish.